BIBLE

STORIES

2

WHAT YOU DON'T HEAR

IN CHURCH!

BIBLE

STORIES

2

WHAT YOU DON'T HEAR

IN CHURCH!

ISBN: 9798598053430

Bible Stories 2

Scripture Quotations are taken from The Holy Bible, Kings James Version,

For permission requests, email the publisher at the address below.

Sfcrj93@gmail.com

<u>Dedication</u>

I want to take a minute to dedicate this book back to God for His inspiration to write all the books that He has allowed me to put to pen! My hearts desire is to be able to put into word the things of Scripture that the Holy Spirit has opened up my mind to the understanding of the "Stories inside the Stories" of those Scriptures. God's Word tells us in 1 Corinthians 10: 11; & Romans 15: 4; "Now all these things happened unto them for examples: and they are written for our admonition, upon whom the ends of the world are come." We are those people at the ends of the world!

I also want to thank my wife, Lynn and my family for their support and love!

Contents

Introduction

This book is the second book in a series of Stories and information from the Bible that has been told and preached millions of times! All this information is very good for living a Christian life, but it is about someone else and their problems! God wants us to understand that God's Word is inexhaustible and will fit into your life and your problems and situations to give you God's solution to those things in your life! Jesus said in [Luke 11: 13] that the Heavenly Father shall give the Holy Spirit to them that ask Him! The Scriptures has "Stories inside the Stories" that will be revealed to you by the Holy Spirit if you seek them in Prayer! Christians seem to set back and want God to take care of all their problems while we do nothing! God's Word tells us that we must do something to get God to do something. **Seek** and you will find! **Knock** and the door will be opened! **Ask** and ye shall receive! God's desire for you is that you will learn to see the solutions that He has already given to you in His Word! I pray that as you read this, God will open your eyes and heart to a lot better life!

<u>We must all Learn!</u>

We as Christians, must grow into "Maturity in Christ," just like we grow into adults in our bodies. We are all creations of God, but we become the Children of God by excepting that Jesus Christ is God Himself come down to earth in flesh to teach us of the Father and died upon the Cross to break the barrier that Adam and Eve caused to separate man from God back in the Garden of Eden! There are things that we must learn and do as Christians to receive the Blessings from God! **We are saved strictly by what Jesus did on the Cross,** but we are blessed and will only go in the Rapture of the Church if we have matured in Christ! [Matthew 25: 1 – 13; Luke 21:34 – 36]! Paul said in [1 Corinthians 13: 11 & 12] that when he was a child, he spoke and acted like a child, but when he became a man, he put away all those childish things! God wants His Children to grow and become someone that He can use for the purpose of Witnessing to everyone that God puts into your pathway and He gives you discernment to tell them about what Jesus has done in your life! It's not your job to knock them in the head and drag them into Church! Jesus said, "If I be lifted up, I'll draw all men to Me"! God, just wants you to tell them about Jesus and what He has done in your Life!

Let's look at how other people in the Bible had to grow and learn!

First of all there was **Adam and Eve!**

Now from the sixth day when God created Adam, God walked and talked with Adam and explained what God expected for him to do and act like! God's Word tells us that as Adam saw the animals created and gave them names, he also noticed that they were paired with a male and female! Adam became very lonely, as he was created in the image and likeness of God being both male and female with the male being dominate! God saw this and as God always does, He used this situation to teach us that He will send a preview of things to come in the future before they get here! Example; from the side of Adam, God put him to sleep and opened his side where God brought forth Adams Bride! Now, God could have spoken Eve into existence but God was giving Adam along with all of us a preview of the future when the Roman soldier penetrated the side of Jesus as He hung on the Cross, sending the tip of the spear up under the ribs, through the lung, into the pericardium bag surrounding the heart, into the heart of Jesus Christ, where Blood and Water would pour out upon the ground! This represented the shedding of Blood and Death [Hebrews 9: 15 & 22] for the remission of sins and the Water represents the Baptism; **"That's the Bride of Christ"! [Acts 2: 38]**

Adam, not being lonely anymore, done what God told him to do and all was well, until Satan, as usual, stuck his nose into what God was doing to try to upset the applecart; so Satan used the Serpent that was in the garden and stood upright and could speak the language of man! The serpent beguiled Eve [Gen. 3: 1] with sweet talk! [You know guys, just like we do our wives when we think that we have done something wrong]. You see, Satan knew that man was a spirit after the *likeness of GOD* and could never die! But our flesh can die! Satan also knew that man did not understand nor even knew about the 2nd death [Rev. 20: 14]! Anyway, Eve fell for all that slick talk and lay with the serpent and then lay with her husband Adam and conceived seed from both of them and bore a set of twins and named them Cain [conceived 1st] and Abel [conceived 2nd] But that's another story for another time! After this thing had taken place, God came to the garden where Adam and Eve were sewing fig leaves together to cover their nakedness, [notice that it was what had taken place that made them see they were naked! [Read Gen. 2: 25 & 3: 6&7], Now at this time [Gen. 3: 8 – 21 & Hebrews 9: 22] God showed Adam and Eve that it would take Death and Blood to cover their sins, "not anything man can do"! Adam learned a hard lesson! My mother would always say "Son, you **will** learn from the "School of Hard Knocks"! Now, How well are you learning? You see, there are so many stories that we have heard about from the Bible, but we never stopped long enough to pray and ask God to reveal the Story inside the Story" by the Holy Spirit that we should have guiding us throughout our lives, if we are

Christians! The Word of GOD has been given to us to help us live our lives the way God wants us to, because God only wants the very best for us! Do you have any children? Do you remember when you were a teenager? Our parents didn't want us to get in trouble in school nor anywhere else. They told us what not to do because they had been where we were before! Just as GOD in the beginning, told Cain when he was mad because God excepted his brother's sacrifice and rejected his sacrifice. GOD told Cain, [Gen. 4:1–11] " If thou doest well, shall thou not be excepted? Well, how do we know how to do well? Simple! Just read the Bible and ask God for understanding, [James 1: 5-8] and He will teach you things that you don't know and will show you what to do that will give you a better life! [John 14: 26-27] You see, what Adam and Eve had done in the Garden of Eden with the Serpent, possessed by Satan was to change the DNA of man that GOD had said when God had made him, that it is good! Now it has been mixed and changed in Cain from what GOD had designed it to be! Now in [James 2: 21 – 22] **James says to also have Faith along with <u>your works</u> [Prayer, Fasting & Studying]** ! .,

[Read; Matthew 7: 12 – 23] Jesus Himself is speaking of things that Men do and He compares us to Trees that bear either Good or Bad Fruit, [Works];

Yes the Garden of Eden was full of trees with fruit to eat and the leaves were for healing of our bodies! But, God's Word uses the word Tree as an example of Man and the way we live our lives! I want you to know that it was not the Apple in the tree! It was the Pair on the ground that became the transgression that built a Barrier wall that separated man from GOD! It was the sexual sin that messed up and changed the DNA of man that GOD had created! It took God Himself to come down to earth in the body of Jesus and die on a Cross and shed His Blood and give His life to break that barrier wall of separation so we can approach the Throne of GOD for Grace and Mercy and redemption of our sins, but we must come through the Mighty name of Jesus Christ to get to the Throne of GOD!!

Abraham and Sarah had Faith!
[Read Hebrews chapter 11]

Quest what! Abraham had to learn a lot of things along with his wife Sarah as they stumbled down the road of life that we, ourselves are trying to travel down each day of our lives! It is all about Choices! We make choices everyday about everything that we do, say and think! Stop! Think about what you base your decisions on! What you have seen? Done before? What you have been told? **Your relationship with GOD is a one on one relationship!** When you learn to talk to God about everything and make your decisions based on the Word of GOD, [The Bible], You will find that God will Bless you in everything that you put your hands to! [Deuteronomy 28: 8] [Read Deuteronomy Chapters 6 & 28]

I know that you think that those Scriptures are for Israel, but God's Word says in [Galatians 3: 29 & Gen. 17: 7] that if ye be in Christ, then ye are a seed of Abraham and heir to the Promise!!!!

Let's look at Abraham and Sarah's lives!

First of all, Abraham had to have Faith to follow GOD's calling and leave the land of the Chaldeans from UR, and everything he was accustom to and leave his family and friends to travel to a foreign land to start over with his life! [Gen. 12: 1 – 5], Abraham started a generational curse [See Bible Stories 1, pg. 142] by lying to the Pharaoh of Egypt and again to Abimelech; [Gen. 12: 10 – 20; & 20: 1 – 11], This followed through Abraham's family in Isaac when he lied about Rebekah being his sister to Abimelech and his men, just as his father Abraham did!

Now, we all know how Jacob lied to his own father to gain the first blessing that belonged to the first born, [Esau] even though Esau sold him his birthright [Genesis 25: 31 – 34; Gen. 27: 19 – 30], We also see this Curse of Lying pass onto the first ten sons of Jacob when they told their father that his son Joseph had been killed by some animal after they had sold him into slavery! [Gen. 37: 13 – 36]. Joseph stopped the Curse of Lying! After 4 generations of it! [Exodus 20:5].

Abraham learned a hard lesson and it came through his wife Sarah just as it did with Adam and Eve; Yes, it had to do with sex, and with anyone other than your God given spouse!!! Sarah grieved because she could not give Abraham, her beloved husband a child, must less a son! She spoke to Abraham and they together decided that God's Promise [Gen. 18: 9 – 15] just was not coming to pass for them! [They lost their Faith!] so Sarah sent her handmaiden Hagar, [an Egyptian, Gen. 16: 3] into Abraham's bed to bare him a son! We all know the story and we all know that the twelve sons of Ishmael, [Gen. 16: 11 – 16] have always been a burden to Israel and all the seed of Abraham, [Galatians 3: 29, & Gen. 17: 7] and will be until the end of time! Remember; What Adam and Eve did, [the Fig leaves] and what Cain did, [sacrifice something he had done instead of Blood and Death] and now

Abraham and Sarah also tried to change God's Word into something that man could do!!! [God said **Sarah** would bear a Son to Abraham]!

So, always remember! We are humans in flesh and will continually make mistakes and sin along the way, but we have a loving GOD through Jesus Christ that may allow us to suffer because of our mistakes, but will forgive us when we ask! What a Savior!

I am only showing you a few of the things that our Brothers and Sisters from the pass, recorded in Bible Scriptures have had to learn!

Let's look at Moses;

Moses was born in a time that God was using to give us a look at what was coming, as God did all throughout the Bible! Moses was born when the King was having all the boy children killed! Just as it was when Jesus was born, remember? Moses was born a poor Hebrew, but grew up as a rich Egyptian, ran away to become a Hebrew living in the wilderness happy with a wife and another family! What kind of lessons do you think that he learned from all those life changes? God had told Abraham that the children of Israel could be in captivity for four hundred years, [Gen. 15: 13 – 14] The Scriptures tell us that Moses had a speech impairment like a studder! The four hundred years had passed and God wanted Moses to go back and lead the Children of Israel out of Egypt! Moses made excuses to God about why he didn't want to do that! He probably said " I ccccan't spspspeak vvvery gggood! With his studder!

Now, God could have healed him of his problem, but I think that God wants us to see that sometimes God wants us to see through these Scriptures that God will be with us in all that we do in our servanthood to Him with all of our physical problems and weakness of mind! [Fear and lack of Faith].

Now, I know that Preachers will tell you that God don't get mad at us, but look at [Exodus 4: 20 – 24] Where God sought to Kill Moses!! And in [Exodus 32: 8 - 10] where God got mad at Israel and started to kill them all and start over with Moses! [Read, Deuteronomy 28: 14 – 68], about the Curses that God will allow to come upon a nation and people if they turned away from GOD! God did kill Moses at the end upon Mt. Nebo, at the top of Pisgah! [Read; Deuteronomy 34: 5 – 7]. Vs. 7 says that Moses was a 120 years old and his eyes was not dim, nor his natural force abated when **he died according to the Word of the LORD!**

[Proverbs 9: 10] tells us that the Fear of the Lord is the beginning of Wisdom:

God doesn't want us to Fear Him as to be afraid of Him all of the time, but He wants us to understand that **He is GOD and His will shall be done!**

So, just as Moses learned, we must learn to follow God's Word just as it

says! When we decide to change it to suit our desires, we will need to pay a price as Moses did! God told him to speak to the rock for water, but Moses struck it in anger because of the Children of Israel were complaining! I can understand how he felt, but we must not loose our temper and do things in anger and out of control! Anything that takes control of your mind and causes our actions to vary from God's Word is a spirit of control, [Jezebel spirit, if it's a person] [Rev. 2: 18 – 29] and [Pharmacia spirit] [Pharmaceuticals] if it is taken like a Drug to control a person! We in America today are seeing that Jezebel spirit as our government is trying to see how far they can go to control the people of the United States, using The Virus and

Money as a tool to do so! We see this spirit in our Churches in people that start to take control of everything that is going on in the Church! Remember, what God said in Rev. 2: 22; that He will send you into the Great Tribulations if you don't stand up against this spirit of control! " That means that you will be a part of the Foolish Virgins and **not** go in the Rapture"!

Moses did not get to go into the Promised Land!

How are you doing? I Pray that you will learn the **Stories inside the Stories** of God's Word and see where you need to change!

Let's look at King David!

Now if you have read my 2nd book that God allowed me to get published; "David, King of Israel", you will already know that David's father was Jesse, but Jesse's wife was not David's mother! [1 Samuel 16: 10 & 11; 17: 12 - 14; 2 Samuel 10: 1 – 2; 17: 25; 1 Chronicles 2: 13 – 16; 19: 1 – 2;

David tells us;

Psalm 51: 5

5 Behold, I was shapen in iniquity; and in sin did my mother conceive me.

Hebrews 13: 4

4 Marriage is honourable in all, and the bed undefiled: but whoremongers and adulterers God will judge.

Psalm 69: 8

[8] I am become a stranger unto my brethren, and an alien unto my mother's children.

David was allowed to live by Nahash, King of the Children of Ammon, as he did not kill David at his birth! David's brothers hated him and made him work as a servant tending a flock of sheep! The Jewish Talmud tells us that they made him eat at a small table in the corner by himself!

What a hard life for a boy to be raised in! David loved God and Prayed and Sang Praises to God, all the time! [1 Samuel 13: 14; A man after GOD's own Heart! David made a lot of mistakes, but He always repented, learned from his mistakes and served God to the best of his heart!

David looked at Bathsheba taking a bath and took her and had her husband killed and God took their child! Reading about David teaches us a lot about our own lives and how God is just waiting for us to repent and find forgiveness from the Throne of GOD!

We learn from God's Word how we should live and then the Flesh takes over and the Heart wants what the Heart wants! So, there is a battle in our minds what to do, but only with the Holy Spirit can we fight these battles and be victorious!

Let's take a look at Daniel!

Israel continued to sin against God and God allowed Babylon to come against them and take captives back to Babylon! Daniel and the three Hebrew children were in that group of people taken to Babylon. Now God always put a Prophet with his people and God left the Prophet Jeremiah in Israel, Ezekiel was sent to the land of the Chaldeans near the city of UR, from where God called Abraham out from. God had to train Daniel to be a Prophet to the Jews in Babylon! [just as God through the Prophet Elijah taught Elisha to see what the Spirit of GOD was doing! [II Kings 2: 9 – 11], **A Prophet must have the Gift from GOD to see what the Holy Spirit is doing and saying!!**

Now Daniel was a young man when he was taken to Babylon, and he loved God to the point that he was willing to pay the price of death, if necessary, to serve GOD and not worship any Idols!

As we see in God's Word that after being tested, Daniel and the three Hebrew children that was with Daniel was blessed by God with skill in learning and Wisdom, [Daniel 1: 17; James 1:5-7] and Daniel was given the understanding of all Visions and Dreams also.

In Daniel chapters 2 & 4 King Nebuchadnezzar had dreams that no one could give the interpretation of, except Daniel! But wait; The Kings dream in chapter 4 was about the King being a Great Tree that was cut down! Or was it? God was teaching Daniel that as the Prophet Isaiah had said that Before ye ask, God will answer thee! God knew that in the future that Daniel would ask of God, what shall befall my people as Daniel had heard that Jerusalem's walls were torn down and the city was in disarray and that the Prophet Jeremiah had prophesied that the people of Israel that were taken to Babylon would be there for 70 years and they had been there for 68 years at that time! So, God gave the King, "Ole Neb" a dream to warn him that if he did not change his attitude about his greatness, that God would cut him down like the tree in the dream and God did make him drop to all fours and eat grass for 7 years. Also God was teaching Daniel that in about 600 years later, that God would come down to earth through the body of Jesus and Israel would reject Him and they would be cut down for 2000 years before GOD would restore them back into a nation, just as God did will King Nebuchadnezzar!

Just as Daniel and all these other men that God used in past times had to learn GOD's Word and God's ways, we as Christians, must learn to watch and listen to the Holy Spirit as He guides us down the paths that God has set before us to follow!

Where do you stand in your walk?

Are you studying God's Word and listening? Or are you just living a good life, thinking that's all you must do?

Your Call, Choose well!

Blessings upon you is my prayer!

What happens after Death? A Study of Paradise!

In our last Bible Study, there was a question; What happens after we die? So let's look at what the Bible says. I know that most of the preachers will tell you that when we die, that we go to Heaven! That is not what God's Word says! The preachers of this last Church age, The Laodicean Church age that we are in are teaching a theology of Henry Ward Beecher, from the mid to late 1800's and not the method or theology of Johnathan Edwards from the 1740's when he preached the sermon, " Sinners in the hands of an Angry God!". This is because they are preaching the truth, but they are putting a slight twist to it, just as Satan did in the wilderness with his temptation of Christ! We as followers of Christ need to learn the God Head and understand the Trinity of GOD! The Father, The Son and The Holy Ghost! You see, we of this Church age like to hear of the good things like, We learn of God through the Son, Jesus, the love, Grace and Mercy of God! We learn of the Teaching and Guidance of God through the Holy Ghost! **But,** we don't like to hear or talk about the Father because He is the Authority that has placed Rules such as the Commandments and Statues spoken of in Deuteronomy chapters 6 & 28 that lays out a life for us to live before God the Father that He has proclaimed that His children would live before Him to be Blessed! The only way to go to Heaven is to accept what God did through the flesh of Jesus Christ on the Cross! But when you Truly accept salvation through Jesus, there will be a change in your actions, words and Works! God's Word tells us that the Laodicean Church would be lukewarm and would not get cold nor hot for God and He would spew them out of His mouth, [Vomit], But that's a story and lesson for another time! Anyway, as I was saying, We have changed the way we look at God so we can live the way that we want to and do the things that we want to do!

Isaiah 28: 9 – 12

⁹ Whom shall he teach knowledge? and whom shall he make to understand doctrine? them that are weaned from the milk, and drawn from the breasts.

¹⁰ For precept must be upon precept, precept upon precept; line upon line, line upon line; here a little, and there a little:

¹¹ For with stammering lips and another tongue will he speak to this people.

¹² To whom he said, This is the rest wherewith ye may cause the weary to rest; and this is the refreshing: yet they would not hear.

** Explanation **

We perceive [precept upon precept] the scriptures [Line upon Line] and little by little we change the scriptures in our minds and hearts to what we want them to be, so we can feel good doing what we want to do!!

Now that we understand what has happened, we understand why Jesus never said anything about the ministry in His parable about the 10 virgins! Jesus knew what the ministry would be like in the last days! I have said all of this to explain what the Word of God says in;

Ephesians 4: 11 – 13

¹¹ And he gave some, apostles; and some, prophets; and some, evangelists; and some, pastors and teachers;

¹² For the perfecting of the saints, for the work of the ministry, for the edifying of the body of Christ:

¹³ Till we all come in the unity of the faith, and of the knowledge of the Son of God, unto a perfect man, unto the

measure of the stature of the fulness of
Christ:

¹⁴ That we henceforth be no more
children, tossed to and fro, and carried
about with every wind of doctrine, by the
sleight of men, and cunning craftiness,
whereby they lie in wait to deceive;

¹⁵ But speaking the truth in love, may
grow up into him in all things, which is
the head, even Christ:

My job and all minister's jobs are to
Perfect the Saints!!!

Refer back onto my teachings on "Where
are the Ministers"!

There are two deaths spoken of in the
Bible. Of the flesh = 1st death. [Romans

5: 12] Of the spirit = 2nd death. [Rev. 20: 14]

Ps. 6: 5

5 For in death there is no remembrance of thee: in the grave who shall give thee thanks?

- In the Grave, we [God's Children] sleep in peace and in the presence of GOD [He is Omni-present] until the Rapture! [1 Thessalonians 4: 14]*

Ps. 68: 20

20 He that is our God is the God of salvation; and unto GOD the Lord belong the issues from death.

- The issues of death and time of rest in death were set up before the beginning of time by God's plan! The Bible states that the Lost Souls would remain in Hell, [just like the

Rich man in Jesus's parable about Lazarus] until the Great White Throne Judgement where they will be Judged by their works and placed back into Hell and Hell will be cast into the Lake of Fire! **This is the Second Death!** Rev. 20: 14.

Ps. 89: 48

[48] What man is he that liveth, and shall not see death? shall he deliver his soul from the hand of the grave? Selah.

- Only God can resurrect the dead and He will do that at the appointed time!
- There has already been one resurrection, The first 12 Elders, [Matthew 27: 52] and there will be another resurrection when the taking away of the Church, [Rapture], when the dead in Christ shall rise first and then those of us that are alive and remain shall be

changed in a twinkling of an eye!
The second 12 Elders making a
total of the 24 Elders in Heaven
sitting around the Throne of GOD! [
Rev. 5: 8; 1 Corinthians 15: 51 –
58] and   [1 Thessalonians 4:
14 – 18]

Romans 6: 9 – 10

[9] Knowing that Christ being raised from
the dead dieth no more; death hath no
more dominion over him.

[10] For in that he died, he died unto sin
once: but in that he liveth, he liveth unto
God.

- God is telling us that all God's
  Children will be like His Son Jesus
  in that we will not face the second
  death! [Rev. 3: 21].

1 Corinthians 15: 51 – 58

[51] Behold, I shew you a mystery; We shall not all sleep, but **we shall all be changed,**

[52] **In a moment, in the twinkling of an eye,** at the **last trump**: for the trumpet shall sound, and **the dead shall be raised incorruptible,** and we shall be changed.

[53] For this corruptible must put on incorruption, and this mortal must put on immortality.

[54] So when this corruptible shall have put on incorruption, and this mortal shall have put on immortality, then shall be brought to pass the saying that is written, Death is swallowed up in victory.

[55] O death, where is thy sting? O grave, where is thy victory?

[56] The sting of death is sin; and the strength of sin is the law.

[57] But thanks be to God, which giveth us the victory through our Lord Jesus Christ.

[58] Therefore, my beloved brethren, be ye stedfast, unmoveable, always abounding in the work of the Lord, forasmuch as ye know that your labour is not in vain in the Lord.

- Again I say to you that if you be in Christ, your soul will after death be in Paradise [asleep in the Presence of God, at rest until the calling away] God's Word does not tell us that God will send us back to the grave again to arise at the coming of our Lord to take His Bride to heaven! After this life, time is no more. Just like it is now in the presence of God! There is only time in this world, not beyond it!

Hebrews 2:9-10

[9] But we see Jesus, who was made a little lower than the angels for the suffering of death, crowned with glory and honour; that he by the grace of God should taste death for every man.

[10] For it became him, for whom are all things, and by whom are all things, in bringing many sons unto glory, to make the captain of their salvation perfect through sufferings.

- God's Word is telling us that because we accepted what Jesus did on the Cross, we will not have to face the second death! [1 peter 3: 18 & John 3: 16]

Hebrews 11: 5

[5] By faith Enoch was translated that he should not see death; and was not found, because God had translated him: for before his translation he had this testimony, that he pleased God.

- Enoch was a typification of the Bride of Christ! He never saw the first death of the flesh !

1 John 5: 16

[16] If any man see his brother sin a sin which is not unto death, he shall ask, and he shall give him life for them that sin not unto death. There is a sin unto death: I do not say that he shall pray for it.

[17] All unrighteousness is sin: and there is a sin not unto death.

[18] We know that whosoever is born of God sinneth not; but he that is begotten

of God keepeth himself, and that wicked one toucheth him not.

[19] And we know that we are of God, and the whole world lieth in wickedness.

[20] And we know that the Son of God is come, and hath given us an understanding, that we may know him that is true, and we are in him that is true, even in his Son Jesus Christ. This is the true God, and eternal life.

- There are two kind of sins; Sins of Commission = sins we commit against God that will take us into the second death and the Sin of Omission = sin of not doing what God ask us to do, like witnessing to someone or taking some family some groceries or praying for someone that God puts on your heart. These you will have to answer for at the Judgement Seat of Christ! 2 Corinthians 5: 10!

Revelation 20: 6

¹¹ And I saw a great white throne, and him that sat on it, from whose face the earth and the heaven fled away; and there was found no place for them.

¹² And I saw the dead, small and great, stand before God; and the books were opened: and another book was opened, which is the book of life: and the dead were judged out of those things which were written in the books, according to their works.

¹³ And the sea gave up the dead which were in it; and death and hell delivered up the dead which were in them: and they were judged every man according to their works.

¹⁴ And death and hell were cast into the lake of fire. This is the second death.

¹⁵ And whosoever was not found written in the book of life was cast into the lake of fire.

Notes

Wake up Church!
And act like the Church Should!

John 16:25

25 These things have I spoken unto you in proverbs [c] : but the time cometh, when I shall no more speak unto you in proverbs, but I shall shew you plainly of the Father. [1]

2 Thessalonians 2:3

3 Let no man deceive you by any means: for *that day shall not come* , except there come a falling away first, and that man of sin be revealed, the son of perdition; [2]

Luke 12:42-43

42 And the Lord said, Who then is that faithful and wise steward, whom *his* lord shall make ruler over his household, to give *them their* portion of meat in due season? 43 Blessed *is* that servant, whom his lord when he cometh shall find so doing. 3

There are 285 denominations of Churches in America!

Luke 11:17

17 But he, knowing their thoughts, said unto them, Every kingdom divided against itself is brought to desolation; and a house *divided* against a house falleth. 4

____

I John 4: 1-6

¹ Beloved, believe not every spirit, but try the spirits whether they are of God: because many false prophets are gone out into the world. ² Hereby know ye the Spirit of God: Every spirit that confesseth that Jesus Christ is come in the flesh is of God: ³ And every spirit that confesseth not that Jesus Christ is come in the flesh is not of God: and this is that *spirit* of antichrist, whereof ye have heard that it should come; and even now already is it in the world. ⁴ Ye are of God, little children, and have overcome them: because greater is he that is in you, than he that is in the world. ⁵ They are of the world: therefore speak they of the world, and the world heareth them. ⁶ We are of God: he that knoweth God heareth us; he that is not of God heareth not us. Hereby know we the spirit of truth, and the spirit of error.

{ I want you to know that we are the children of GOD, but we need to wake up and start acting like it!}

Matthew 18:18

18 Verily I say unto you, Whatsoever ye shall bind on earth shall be bound in heaven: and whatsoever ye shall loose on earth shall be loosed in heaven. 5

Matthew 21: 21&22

21 Jesus answered and said unto them, Verily I say unto you, If ye have faith, and doubt not, ye shall not only do this *which is done* to the fig tree, but also if ye shall say unto this mountain, Be thou removed, and be thou cast into the sea; it shall be done. **22 And all things,**

____

whatsoever ye shall ask in prayer, believing, ye shall receive. [6]

Revelations 3: 14-16

[14] And unto the angel of the church of the Laodiceans [a] write; These things saith the Amen, the faithful and true witness, **the beginning of the creation of God;** [15] I know thy works, that thou art neither cold nor hot: I would thou wert cold or hot. [16] So then because thou art lukewarm, and neither cold nor hot, I will spue thee out of my mouth. [7]

[There will many preachers that will answer to GOD for allowing themselves

____

to bow to Church Doctrines and Creeds and not preaching the Word of GOD!]

Rev. 5:6

6 And I beheld, and, lo, in the midst of the throne and of the four beasts, and in the midst of the elders, stood a Lamb as it had been slain, having seven horns and seven eyes, which are the seven Spirits of God sent forth into all the earth. 8

Revelations 2: 18-22

18 And unto the angel of the church in Thyatira write; These things saith the Son of God, who hath his eyes like unto a flame of fire, and his feet *are* like fine brass; 19 I know thy works, and charity, and service, and faith, and thy patience,

____

and thy works; and the last *to be* more than the first. **20 Notwithstanding I have a few things against thee, because thou sufferest that woman Jezebel,** which calleth herself a prophetess, to teach and to seduce my servants to commit fornication, and to eat things sacrificed unto idols. 21 And I gave her space to repent of her fornication; and she repented not. 22 Behold, I will cast her into a bed, and **them that commit adultery with her into great tribulation,** except they repent of their deeds. 9

[It is time for the Church to wake up! Jesus Christ is soon coming and **we are playing Church!** Our Job is to Witness to the world about Jesus, by our Lives, Conversations and our non-tolerance of

Evil! If the churches would come together and stand up to the government through our combined vote and our voices, this would be a different world!]

[That great falling away that GOD's Word speaks of is "The Church"!!! Imagine that!]

<u>Are we hiding from the presence of God</u>
<u>In the midst of His Blessings.</u>

Genesis 3: 8-9

⁸ And they heard the voice of the LORD God walking in the garden in the cool ^d of the day: and Adam and his wife hid themselves from the presence of the LORD God amongst the trees of the garden.

⁹ And the LORD God called unto Adam, and said unto him, Where *art* thou?

** God's Word tells us that they were in the Garden of Eden, still enjoying the blessings of GOD while they were sowing fig leaves together to try to cover up their Sin!

Numbers 14: 30 -33

³⁰ Doubtless ye shall not come into the land, concerning which I sware to make you dwell therein, save Caleb the son of Jephunneh, and Joshua the son of Nun.

³¹ But your little ones, which ye said should be a prey, them will I bring in, and they shall know the land which ye have despised.

³² But as for you, your carcases, they shall fall in this wilderness.

³³ And your children shall wander in the wilderness forty years, and bear your whoredoms, until your carcases be wasted in the wilderness.

** Because of their showing no faith in GOD, they were doomed to walk through the wilderness until all of them from 20 yrs. Old and up were dead! Now, GOD allowed them to live under God's blessings of; A pillar of Fire by night; Bread from the sky in the morning, and Meat from the sky in the Evenings; A Cloud by day; No sick among them; Their Clothes and Shoes never wore out for 40 years!

*** And they Died LOST! **

I Corinthians 10: 11

11 Now all these things happened unto them for examples [b] : and they are written for our admonition, upon whom the ends of the world are come. 12 Wherefore let him that thinketh he standeth take heed lest he fall. 13 There hath no temptation taken you but such as is common to man: but God *is* faithful, who will not suffer you to be tempted above that ye are able;

---

but will with the temptation also make a way to escape, that ye may be able to bear *it* . [14] Wherefore, my dearly beloved, flee from idolatry. [10]

What idols do we have in our lives?

What controls your time!! Your Job?, Home?,

I Corinthians 10: 23

[23] All things are lawful for me, but all things are not expedient: all things are lawful for me, but all things edify not. [11]

God wants to Bless each one of His children **But** God wants us to give Him the Credit, praise & glory!

God also wants us to be a witness of His Love and Grace

Through our lives and testimony !!

Let God lead you with His Spirit thru His Word!!

James 4: 14-15

14 Whereas ye know not what *shall be* on the morrow. For what *is* your life? It is even a vapour, that appeareth for a little time, and then vanisheth away. 15 For that ye *ought* to say, **If the Lord will, we shall live, and do this, or that. 12**

Jonah 1: 1-3

[1] Now the word of the LORD came unto
Jonah [a] the son of Amittai,
saying, [2] Arise, go to Nineveh, that
great city, and cry against it; for their
wickedness is come up before
me. [3] But Jonah rose up to flee unto
Tarshish from the presence of the LORD,
and went down to Joppa; and he found
a ship going to Tarshish: so he paid the
fare thereof, and went down into it, to
go with them unto Tarshish from the
presence of the LORD.

We want to live in & under God's
blessings and love, but we don't want to

____

live as God's word lays it out for us to live.

We don't want to do what God has asked us to do!

{ Sins of Omission !! }

Jonah done what God asked but with a bad attitude!!

We want to take credit for all that God has done for us!

Daniel 4: 30-37
30 The king spake, and said, Is not this great Babylon, that **I** have built for the house of the kingdom by the might of **my power**, and for the honour of **my majesty?** 31 While the word *was* in the king's mouth, there fell a voice from heaven, *saying* , O king Nebuchadnezzar, to thee it is spoken;

The kingdom is departed from thee. [32] And they shall drive thee from men, and thy dwelling *shall be* with the beasts of the field: they shall make thee to eat grass as oxen, and seven times shall pass over thee, until thou know that the **most High ruleth in the kingdom of men**, and giveth it to whomsoever he will. [33] The same hour was the thing fulfilled upon Nebuchadnezzar: and he was driven from men, and did eat grass as oxen, and his body was wet with the dew of heaven, till his hairs were grown like eagles' *feathers* , and his nails like birds' *claws* . [34] And at the end of the days I Nebuchadnezzar lifted up mine eyes unto heaven, and mine understanding returned unto me, and I blessed the most High, and I praised and honoured him that liveth for ever, whose dominion *is* an everlasting dominion, and his kingdom *is* from generation to generation: 35 And all the inhabitants of the earth *are* reputed as nothing: and he doeth according to his will in the army of heaven, and *among* the inhabitants of the earth: and none can stay his hand, or say unto him, What doest thou? 36 At the same time my reason returned unto me; and for the glory of my kingdom, mine honour and brightness returned unto me; and my counsellors and my lords sought unto me; and I was established in my kingdom, and excellent majesty was added unto me. 37 Now I Nebuchadnezzar praise and extol and honour the King of heaven, all whose works *are* truth, and his ways judgment:

and those that walk in pride he is able to abase.

   **Why do you think that God gave Pastors & Teachers ?

   Ephesians 4: 9-13

⁹ (Now that he ascended, what is it but that he also descended first into the lower parts of the earth? ¹⁰ He that descended is the same also that ascended up far above all heavens, that he might fill ᶜ all things.) ¹¹ And he gave some, apostles; and some, prophets; and some, evangelists; and some, pastors and teachers; ¹² **For the perfecting of the saints, for the work of the ministry, for the edifying of the**

____

body of Christ: [13] **Till we all come in** [d] **The unity of the faith, and of the knowledge of the Son of God, unto a perfect man, unto the measure of the stature of the fulness of Christ:** [13]

** The Teres will hide in the mist of the wheat, and enjoy the fertilizers and loose soil the farmer put into the ground and worked hard to plow the field and prepare the soil for the wheat!

** The 80 / 20 Rule **

80% of all the work is done by 20% of the people!

** What group do you fit in?

____

Marks on the Foreheads and hands!

[God's Word tells us that from the beginning that God used marks to teach us about Him and to explain how important that marks on our bodies, tags on our cars/trucks, signs on or about our homes are! From the beginning God set a mark upon Cain;]

Gen. 4:15

15 And the LORD said unto him, Therefore whosoever slayeth Cain, vengeance shall be taken on him sevenfold. And the LORD set a mark upon Cain, lest any finding him should kill him.

[God had Moses to put a mark of lambs blood on the lintel and doorposts of their homes; {this is symbolic of the forehead and hands} to avert the Angel of Death while they were in Egypt.]

[God told Moses to have the people to put His Word before their eyes as frontlets and on their hands to remind them to always "Love the Lord with all your Hearts" and to keep His laws.]

Deut. 6:4-9

4 Hear, O Israel: The LORD our God *is* one LORD: 5 And thou shalt love the LORD thy God with all thine heart, and with all thy soul, and with all thy might. 6 And these words, which I

command thee this day, shall be in thine heart: 7 And thou shalt teach them diligently unto thy children, and shalt talk of them when thou sittest in thine house, and when thou walkest by the way, and when thou liest down, and when thou risest up. 8 And thou shalt bind them for a sign upon thine hand, and they shall be as frontlets between thine eyes. 9 And thou shalt write them upon the posts of thy house, and on thy gates.

[God became very angry when David numbered the people.]

II Samuel 24: 10-12

10 And David's heart smote him after that he had numbered the people. And David said unto the LORD, I have sinned greatly in that I have done: and now, I

beseech thee, O LORD, take away the iniquity of thy servant; for I have done very foolishly. ¹¹ For when David was up in the morning, the word of the LORD came unto the prophet Gad, David's seer, saying, ¹² Go and say unto David, Thus saith the LORD, I offer thee three *things* ; choose thee one of them, that I may *do it* unto thee.

[God told Ezekiel to put a mark onto the foreheads of certain men.]

Ezekiel 9:4-6

⁴ And the LORD said unto him, Go through the midst of the city, through the midst of Jerusalem, and set a mark [b] upon the foreheads of the men that sigh and that cry for all the

---

abominations that be done in the midst thereof.

⁵ And to the others he said in mine hearing ᶜ , Go ye after him through the city, and smite: let not your eye spare, neither have ye pity: ⁶ Slay utterly ᵈ old *and* young, both maids, and little children, and women: but come not near any man upon whom *is* the mark; and begin at my sanctuary. Then they began at the ancient men which *were* before the house.

[Satan can not create, he can only copy what God has already done and pervert that thing, as is his ways about all that he does. The Word of God says that the antichrist will give all that will except him or join him in the hand of fellowship a mark to identify them and those

____

without it cannot buy nor sell to live. The mark is the number of man that is the number 6, and his name will workout through Jewish Math to the number 666.]

[I believe, {by all that God has shown to me through His Word and by His peace in my heart about the subject} that the mark of the beast will be that they will believe that the antichrist is god; Mark in the Head; or they will take the right hand of fellowship so they will not be killed and they will be able to buy food and other needs; Mark in the Hand;]

[God's Word tells us in the book of Revelation that God will seal the 144,000 Jews in their foreheads]

Rev. 7: 3&4

³ Saying, Hurt not the earth, neither the sea, nor the trees, till we have sealed the servants of our God in their foreheads. ⁴ And I heard the number of them which were sealed: *and there were* sealed an hundred *and* forty *and* four thousand of all the tribes of the children of Israel.

[The Mark of the Beast is not something that we { God's Church} need to worry about. We will already be in Heaven and will not see God's wrath nor will we see the antichrist as he shows up <u>after</u> the Rapture of God's Church!] [Matthew 24: 14 & 15]

[God used marks and symbols all throughout the old testament and Jesus spoke in proverbs and parables to explain what he was speaking about, and the common people heard Him gladly.]

[God gives us His Ministers to teach us of his Word that we may grow into mature children and understand His Word.]

Ephesians 4: 11-15

11 And he gave some, apostles; and some, prophets; and some, evangelists; and some, pastors and teachers; 12 For the perfecting of the saints, for the work of the ministry, for the edifying of the body of Christ: 13 Till we all come

in ^d the unity of the faith, and of the knowledge of the Son of God, unto a perfect man, unto the measure of the stature of the fulness of Christ: ¹⁴ That we *henceforth* be no more children, tossed to and fro, and carried about with every wind of doctrine, by the sleight of men, *and* cunning craftiness, whereby they lie in wait to deceive; ¹⁵ But speaking the truth in love, may grow up into him in all things, which is the head, *even* Christ:

"Peter Pan Christians"

" People who won't grow up"
[Mature in Christ!]
Hebrews 5: 12 - 14

[12] For when for the time ye ought to be teachers, ye have need that one teach you again which *be* the first principles of the oracles of God; and are become such as have need of milk, and not of strong meat. [13] For every one that useth milk *is* unskilful in the word of righteousness: for he is a babe. [14] **But strong meat belongeth to them that are of full age** [c] , *even* those who by reason of use have their senses exercised to discern both good and evil. [14]

" They are caught up in the Cares of Life"

" Growing requires work"

I Peter 2: 1 - 12

[1] Wherefore laying aside all malice, and all guile, and hypocrisies, and envies, and all evil speakings, [2] As newborn babes, desire the sincere milk of the word, that ye may grow thereby: [3] If so be ye have tasted that the Lord *is* gracious.

[4] To whom coming, *as unto* a living stone, disallowed indeed of men, but chosen of God, *and* precious, [5] Ye also, as lively stones, are built up a spiritual house, an holy priesthood, to offer up spiritual sacrifices, acceptable to God by Jesus Christ. [6] Wherefore also it is contained in the scripture, Behold, I lay in Sion a chief corner stone, elect,

precious: and he that believeth on him shall not be confounded. [7] Unto you therefore which believe *he is* precious [a] : but unto them which be disobedient, the stone which the builders disallowed, the same is made the head of the corner, [8] And a stone of stumbling, and a rock of offence, *even to them* which stumble at the word, being disobedient: whereunto also they were appointed. [9] **But ye *are* a chosen generation, a royal priesthood, an holy nation, a peculiar [b] people; that ye should shew forth the praises of him who hath called you out of darkness into his marvellous light:** [10] Which in time past *were* not a people, but *are* now the people of God: which had not obtained mercy, but now have obtained mercy. [11] Dearly beloved, I beseech *you* as strangers and pilgrims, abstain from

____

fleshly lusts, which war against the
soul; [12] Having your conversation
honest among the Gentiles: that,
whereas [c] they speak against you as
evildoers, **they may by _your_ good
works, which they shall behold, glorify
God in the day of visitation.**

The Two Adams and their Brides

The story inside the Story

Genesis 2: 20 – 25

[20] And Adam gave names to all cattle, and to the fowl of the air, and to every beast of the field; but for Adam there was not found an help meet for him.

[21] And the LORD God caused a deep sleep to fall upon Adam, and he slept: and he took one of his ribs, and closed up the flesh instead thereof;

[22] And the rib, which the LORD God had taken from man, made he a woman, and brought her unto the man.

[23] And Adam said, This is now bone of my bones, and flesh of my flesh: she shall be called Woman, because she was taken out of Man.

^{24} Therefore shall a man leave his father and his mother, and shall cleave unto his wife: and they shall be one flesh.

^{25} And they were both naked, the man and his wife, and were not ashamed.

** Now, from the beginning, God created the first Adam. God saw that man could not live as God did even though Adam was in the likeness and image of God! God put Adam asleep and removed a rib. God then created woman and removed the female part from Adam! [man]. Adam called her Eve, because she, [female] would bear the children. She [female] had the caring, home making, feeling, compassionate, sensitiveness side of God **that was in Adam, [man] at creation.** God removed more than a rib from Adam! God removed all feminist feelings and actions from him! God then brought Eve to Adam and blessed them. Adam, like all men, are not whole in the way that they think, without the advise of their wives! Men must learn to discuss situations with their wives, before they make a decision that will effect their family. God's Word tells us that together we are one! GOD don't make mistakes! God separated female from the male, so if you don't know which bathroom to use, you have a perverted demonic spirit dealing with you!!!

Back to the Story! God opened Adam's side and took out a Bride for Adam!

Now, Adam and his Lovely wife Eve, only had to keep a few Commandments that GOD had told them to do and not to do. They messed that up, just like all the rest of us do all the time! That little mess up, built a barrier wall between man and GOD!

" It's not very smart to make GOD mad at yourself" There's a name for that, it's called **"Stupid"** !!!

As Paul Harvey used to say, "Now, Here's the rest of the story"

John 19: 31 – 37

31 The Jews therefore, because it was the preparation that the bodies should not remain upon the cross on the sabbath day, (for that sabbath day was a high day,) besought Pilate that their legs might be broken, and that they might be taken away.

32 Then came the soldiers, and brake the legs of the first, and of the other which was crucified with him.

33 But when they came to Jesus, and saw that he was dead already, they brake not his legs:

34 But one of the soldiers with a spear pierced his side, and forthwith came there out **blood and water.**

35 And he that saw it bare record, and his record is true: and he knoweth that he saith true, that ye might believe.

36 For these things were done, that the scripture should be fulfilled, A bone of him shall not be broken.

37 And again another scripture saith, They shall look on him whom they pierced.

GOD, from the beginning knew that man could not live by His Laws, Statutes and Commandments! [Deuteronomy 6: 1 – 9]. So, because God loved us so much, He came down to earth, through the body of Jesus, The Christ, The first Adam, and died on the Cross, and upon His death, Jesus kicked a big hole in that barrier wall, stepped into the opening and said, Now, children, you can approach the Throne of GOD boldly, but only by coming through me, **in the name of Jesus!

Now, here's what took place after Jesus had died, the Roman soldiers came to the Crosses and broke the legs of the two thieves that were there so they could not push themselves upward to catch a breath of air, and they died quickly! When they came to Jesus, seeing that He was already dead. They pushed a Roman Spear into His side to make sure. When the spear penetrated Christ's side it went up at an angle into the Heart of Christ! From that wound, came the **Blood** of Redemption and the **Water**, symbolizing the Baptism of The Holy Spirit. In other words, " The Church" that is " **The Bride of Christ"**

I wrote this story to show you how to see, how GOD desires for us to read and see Him through the information in the Bible that He has placed there for us. [I Cor. 10: 11 & Romans 15: 4].

A Roman Spear = A 4' 7" Wooden
handle with a 24" iron shank

With a barb on the tip making it <u>about</u>
6'7" long overall!

Ezekiel

The Vision of the Four Wheels

Chapter 1

1 Now it came to pass in the thirtieth year, in the fourth month, in the fifth day of the month, as I was among the captives by the river of Chebar, that the heavens were opened, and I saw visions of God.

**Ezekiel starts out giving us and understanding that by the opinion of most scholars, he was in his thirtieth year of his ministry. He reports that he was one of the captives that were taken to Babylonia. He states that he was with the captives by the river Chebar! We don't know where that is, but, Vs. 3 tells us that he was somewhere near "Ur in the land of the Chaldeans, the country God called Abraham from. The Heavens opening and he sees GOD in a vision, This means that it was the beginning of Ezekiel's Prophetic Ministry! **

2 In the fifth day of the month, which was the fifth year of king Jehoiachin's captivity,

** Ezekiel had been in captivity for 5 years and all the false prophets in Israel and Judah were prophesying that they would be released in a couple years, [Jer. 28: 3] but, Ezekiel knew what God's prophet Jeremiah had written in a letter to the captive Jews. [Jer. 29: 1-23] **

3 The word of the LORD came expressly unto Ezekiel the priest, the son of Buzi, in the land of the Chaldeans by the river Chebar; and the hand of the LORD was there upon him.

** The Word of the Lord came expressly to Ezekiel, means that there was " No Doubt" [Daniel 10: 20] and as he was in the land of the Chaldeans, means that where ever a person is and they are seeking God's guidance, that GOD is Omni-present and they will find Him! **

4 And I looked, and, behold, a whirlwind came out of the north, a great cloud, and a fire infolding itself, and a brightness was about it, and out of the midst thereof as the colour of amber, out of the midst of the fire.

** And I looked and behold! Means that his vision could be seen! Ezekiel was not imagining this. The Whirlwind he saw was the Holy Spirit seen in [Acts 2: 2], in the upper room, and in [II Kings 2: 1 & 11] Elijah leaves this world. I believe that Ezekiel saw the Cherubim that stands at the Throne of GOD!**

[5] Also out of the midst thereof came the likeness of four living creatures. And this was their appearance; **they had the likeness of a man.**

** We see in chapter 10: 1, that they are Cherubim!

See also [Revelation 4: 7] it describes the Cherubims before the Throne of GOD! **

[6] And every one had four faces, and every one had four wings.

** Notice that the Cherubim before the Throne of GOD, are four individual creatures , but has six wings each! **

[7] And their feet were straight feet; and the sole of their feet was like the sole of a calf's foot: and they sparkled like the colour of burnished brass.

** Their feet were straight, like the feet of an OX. Per vs. 5, they had the likeness of a man, so they had two legs! **

[8] And they had the hands of a man under their wings on their four sides; and they four had their faces and their wings.

** Apparently, these living creatures had the form of a man, with arms and hands underneath the lower set of wings.**

[9] Their wings were joined one to another; they turned not when they went; they went every one straight forward.

** These Creatures did not walk, because they had wheels below them. I watch as our young people are using some sort of ride with two wheels. One on each side and they balance themselves on it and as they lean forward, it goes forward, and so forth backward. **

[10] As for the likeness of their faces, they four had the face of a man, and the face of a lion, on the right side: and they four had the face of an ox on the left side; they four also had the face of an eagle.

** Notice, they have two faces on two sides, left and right! So, was their heads flat on the front and wide enough for four faces? They went straight when they went and turned not! We can connect all this with the Face of the Son of GOD! Who became a man to deliver us back to the Father, The face of the OX in that He sacrificed, [bore the burden of our sins], the Lion shows His sovereignty as GOD and is the Lion of Judah, [Rev. 5: 5], The Eagle, with that of His bearing us on Eagle's wings unto the highest heavens, [Ex. 19: 4; Deut. 32: 11]. **

[11] Thus were their faces: and their wings were stretched upward; two wings of

every one were joined one to another, and two covered their bodies.

** Apparently, They these Cherubim had two wings on the right and left of their bodies, one above the other and the upper wings pointing upward touched the tips together, like we see on the Ark of Covenant forming the Mercy Seat of GOD! **

12 And they went every one straight forward: whither the spirit was to go, they went; and they turned not when they went.

** We as humans, have four sides! Front, Back, Left and Right! We walk straight [Except some of us Wobble a bit as we get older!], If Christians could just learn to follow the Spirit like that! [James 5: 12] tells us to let our yea be yea & your nay be nay! These creatures had a perfect knowledge of direction and

the ability to go where ever the Spirit of
GOD told them to go!**

¹³ As for the likeness of the living
creatures, their appearance was like
burning coals of fire, and like the
appearance of lamps: it went up and
down among the living creatures; and the
fire was bright, and out of the fire went
forth lightning.

** We see here that these creatures, are
covered by the fire and yet, not
consumed by it and by it enhanced with
God's Power to do God's biding.**

¹⁴ And the living creatures ran and
returned as the appearance of a flash of
lightning.

** These boys are Quick! If They think
of a place, they are transported to that
place as through thought and as fast as a
thought travels like a flash of light
through our minds. **

¹⁵ Now as I beheld the living creatures, behold one wheel upon the earth by the living creatures, with his four faces.

** This tells us that one wheel was upon the earth. Vs. 18 says the wheels are full of eyes, are they "Watchers" as spoken of in [Daniel 4:13&17]?**

¹⁶ The appearance of the wheels and their work was like unto the colour of a beryl: and they four had one likeness: and their appearance and their work was as it were a wheel in the middle of a wheel.

** An automobile wheel has two parts, the tire and the medal rim. They both work together and need each other to function in travel and smooth ride. Since the Cherubims were not attached to the wheels, but traveled with them should mean that The "Cherubims" were traveling with "Watchers" as the Holy

One and a Watcher appeared in Daniel's dream in. [Daniel 4: 13 & 17]. **

[17] When they went, they went upon their four sides: and they turned not when they went.

** This suggest that they traveled straight and worked in harmony together! **

[18] As for their rings, they were so high that they were dreadful; and their rings were full of eyes round about them four.

** John the Beloved saw living creatures at Patmos that had eyes before and behind. [Rev. 4: 6]. These eyes are watching as the Cherubim bring Ezekiel Word from GOD that he was moving him from a Priest to a Prophet! **

[19] And when the living creatures went, the wheels went by them: and when the

living creatures were lifted up from the earth, the wheels were lifted up.

** Understand that these Living Creatures were created by God for a purpose. They are a type of angelic being and they are to do whatever God sends them to do, even though they encounter conflicts and obstacles from demonic spirits, they "Get the job done"! The wheels are Watchers, that see everything being done and also see the Glory of GOD! The Cherubim seem to draw knowledge from them! **

[20] Whithersoever the spirit was to go, they went, thither was their spirit to go; and the wheels were lifted up over against them: for the spirit of the living creature was in the wheels.

** We see in the Scriptures, that when the Spirit of God moves, things happen! [Judges 14: 6]. The spirit of these creatures was in the wheels, so they received their instructions from God through the wheels that went with them!**

21 When those went, these went; and when those stood, these stood; and when those were lifted up from the earth, the wheels were lifted up over against them: for the spirit of the living creature was in the wheels.

** I repeat the above statement! **

22 And the likeness of the firmament upon the heads of the living creature was as the colour of the terrible crystal, stretched forth over their heads above.

23 And under the firmament were their wings straight, the one toward the other: every one had two, which covered on this side, and every one had two, which covered on that side, their bodies.

** The firmament is the sky and heavens above,[Gen. 1: 14]. Vs. 9 told us that when they moved, their two top wings pointed upward and the tips touched each other. The bottom two wings were always down and covered their bodies. **

24 And when they went, I heard the noise of their wings, like the noise of great waters, as the voice of the Almighty, the voice of speech, as the noise of an host: when they stood, they let down their wings.

** This chapter does not tell us anything except that the wings only pointed up or straight out. But he heard the sound of their wings. It must have been the sound of the air moving by their wings that sounded like Praises to GOD! [Rev. 19: 6] **

^{25} And there was a voice from the firmament that was over their heads, when they stood, and had let down their wings.

** The voice of GOD! **

^{26} And above the firmament that was over their heads was the likeness of a throne, as the appearance of a sapphire stone: and upon the likeness of the throne was the likeness as the appearance of a man above upon it.

** This verse tells us that God allowed Ezekiel to see the Glorified body of Jesus Christ sitting on the Throne of GOD! **

^{27} And I saw as the colour of amber, as the appearance of fire round about within it, from the appearance of his loins even upward, and from the appearance of his loins even downward, I saw as it were

the appearance of fire, and it had
brightness round about.

** The scriptures teach us that God can
not be seen by man as He is Omni-
Present [everywhere], But we know
that when Jesus came into the upper
room that He did not open the door! He
appeared there in His glorified body as
Ezekiel saw in vs. 26. Moses saw God in
a burning bush, as a flame of fire that
consumed not the bush! [Rev. 19: 12-13]
says that the eyes of Jesus will be as a
flame of fire! Fire burns away the
impurities of things just as the Spirit of
Jesus Christ will remove all of our sins,
if we except Jesus into our hearts and ask
Him to forgive us of all our sins! **

28 As the appearance of the bow that is in
the cloud in the day of rain, so was the
appearance of the brightness round
about. This was the appearance of the
likeness of the glory of the LORD. And

when I saw it, I fell upon my face, and I heard a voice of one that spake.

** [Rev. 4: 2&3] Tells us that John saw the Throne of GOD and there was a rainbow around it with a brightness that is the Glory of the Lord. This denotes who GOD is, and that my people is what GOD wants. He said that He knew us before the foundation of the world, so what He desires for us, is for us to know who and what GOD is in every aspect! When we do, we will live for GOD as never before! **

<u>The Baptist Doctrine of Once Saved always Saved!</u>

** I want to try to examine this Doctrine of the Baptist Church the best way I can per the Word of God! It is and everybody will tell you that it comes from Romans 8: 38 & 39; **

** I don't want to upset anyone by tearing down their faith, but I want to examine this and explain that there is nothing that can separate you from God's Love, but God loves all of His creation! We become Children of GOD only by accepting what Jesus Christ did on the Cross when He died, and when

Jesus's Spirit came down off of the Cross and kicked a hole [opening] into the barrier that Adam and Eve caused to separate us from GOD in the Garden of Eden! Jesus then stepped into that opening and said; Now, you can approach the Throne of GOD to receive Grace, Forgiveness and Mercy, but you must come by Me! [Hebrews 4: 16], for I Am the Way, Truth and the Light and no one cometh unto the Father, but by Me. [John 14: 6]. Now, that being said; let's look at what God's Word says about Eternal Life! **

John 3: 16

16 For God so loved the world, that he gave his only begotten Son, that **whosoever believeth** in him should not perish, but **have everlasting life.**

Romans 8: 38 & 39

³⁸ For **I am persuaded**, that neither death, nor life, nor angels, nor principalities, nor powers, nor things present, nor things to come,

³⁹ Nor height, nor depth, nor any other creature, shall be able to **separate us from the love of God**, which is in Christ Jesus our Lord.

Ezekiel 3: 17 – 21

¹⁷ **Son of man, I have made thee a watchman unto the house of Israel:** therefore hear the word at my mouth, and give them warning from me.

¹⁸ When I say unto the wicked, Thou shalt surely die; and thou givest him not warning, nor speakest to warn the wicked from his wicked way, to save his life; the **same wicked man shall die in his iniquity;** but his blood will I require at thine hand.

¹⁹ Yet if thou warn the wicked, and he turn not from his wickedness, nor from his wicked way, he shall die in his iniquity; but thou hast delivered thy soul.

²⁰ Again, **When a righteous man** doth turn from his righteousness, and commit iniquity, and I lay a stumbling-block before him, he shall die: because thou hast not given him warning, **he shall die in his sin, and his righteousness which he hath done shall not be remembered;** but his blood will I require at thine hand.

²¹ Nevertheless **if thou warn the righteous man, that the righteous sin not, and he doth not sin, he shall surely live**, because he is warned; also thou hast delivered thy soul.

Revelations 2: 5

^{5} Remember therefore from whence thou art fallen, and repent, and do the first works; or else I will come unto thee quickly, and **will remove thy candlestick out of his place, except thou repent.**

Revelations 3: 5 & 6

^{5} **He that overcometh,** the same shall be clothed in white raiment; and **I will not blot out his name out of the book of life,** but I will confess his name before my Father, and before his angels.

^{6} **He that hath an ear, let him hear what the Spirit saith unto the churches.**

** God's Word says that if we sin and repent not, we will die, [the 2nd death, Rev. 20: 11 – 15], GOD doesn't want us to die lost ! [The 1st death of the flesh

], GOD wants us to except Him through Jesus Christ and live as witnesses of what Christ has done for us to the lost world! What will you do? How will you live your life? **

** You know, I have watched for a long time and I realize that people just can't help themselves to keep from adding to what God has told us in His Word! We just seem to want to change things to sound and mean what we want them to sound like and mean what we want them to mean! It's just the Flesh's way of telling God that we want to be free to do what we want to do and the way we want to do things! Look at the world today. We see people everywhere all upset at the way things are today because of the Corona Virus! [and that includes me], We want to go where we want to, whenever we want to and do things like going to a restaurant to eat or travel to see other places or hang out with a group of people! We feel confined and "That" is not what we like! The Prophet Isaiah said;**

Isaiah 28: 9 - 12

[9] Whom shall he teach knowledge? and whom shall he make to understand doctrine? them that are weaned from the milk, and drawn from the breasts.

[10] For precept must be upon precept, **_precept_ upon precept; line upon _line_, line upon line; here a _little_, and there a little:**

[11] For with stammering lips and another tongue will he speak to this people.

[12] To whom he said, This is the rest wherewith ye may cause the weary to

rest; and this is the refreshing: **yet they would not hear.**

** ___Precept___ [What we Perceive in our minds]

** ___Line___ [Scripture giving us what God wants us to do]

** ___Little___ [now with this Scripture and again with that Scripture we change the meaning of God's Word in our minds and hearts to suit our desires so we can live how we want to live!!!].

** and we don't want to hear anybody telling us that we can't do what we want according to God's Word! **

1 Corinthians 14: 21

[20] Brethren, be not children in understanding: howbeit in malice be ye children, but in understanding be men.

[21] In the law it is written, With men of other tongues and other lips will I speak unto this people; and yet for all that will **they not hear me, saith the Lord.**

** Now, this Scripture is when Paul was explaining about speaking in tongues, but as he said, They will not hear what God is telling them through God's Servant! No more than they do now in the Churches and the Pastors are not teaching the Full Truth! We don't want to hear anything that we don't like! **

**We all want to hear the Preacher telling us those things that make us feel good inside and feel like the life we are living is right and all is well, and we are pleasing God with our lifestyle! **

**Please understand that I am not trying to upset anyone nor am I trying to put the Preachers down! I just want to get you to take a look at your lifestyle in the mirror of God's Word and judge for yourselves what you look like! If you walk like a Duck and quack like a Duck and look like a Duck, you must be a Duck! Look at the Lost World. Do you Walk, Talk and Look like the rest of the world? If so, you need to ask God to allow the Holy Spirit to come into your heart and guide you with the Word in getting your life realigned with what God's Word Truly says about how to live! **

John the Baptist could have had it made if he would have just stayed at home and became a Priest and he would have [by Jewish Law] took his father's place as a Priest in the Temple! But John did what God led him to do by the guidance of the Holy Spirit in living in the wilderness eating locust and honey wearing old scratchy clothes made of camel hair! He stood in the midst of the river **crying out to all that would Hear him to get their lives lined up with the Word of God, because the **Messiah was Coming!!****

**** Where are we now!** Drawing nearer to the **Calling away of the Church, [Rapture],** than we have ever been! And **just as it was then, People just will not hear!**

You know; I love all my Pastor and Minster friends and I know that they have told me that they can't preach nor teach like I do because the people would fire them and they would not have a job! I don't work for any Church nor do I allow anyone to dictate to me what I speak about! I am 73 years old and I am only going to speak what GOD shows and tells me to do or speak! I am looking for my Jesus to call us home very soon and I don't plan on being in that group of "Foolish Virgins" [Matthew 25: 1 – 13], [Christians that are not ready to go in the Rapture that must go into the Tribulation and die for Christ, "Saints under the Alter"], [Rev. 6: 8 – 11] **

1 Corinthians 2: 14 – 16

14 But the natural man receiveth not the things of the Spirit of God: for they are foolishness unto him: neither can he know them, because they are spiritually discerned.

15 But he that is spiritual judgeth all things, yet he himself is judged of no man.

¹⁶ For who hath known the mind of the Lord, that he may instruct him? but we have the mind of Christ.

1 Corinthians 3: 1 – 3

3 And I, brethren, could not speak unto you as unto spiritual, but as unto carnal, even as unto babes in Christ.

² I have fed you with milk, and not with meat: for hitherto ye were not able to bear it, neither yet now are ye able.

³ For ye are yet carnal: for whereas there is among you envying, and strife, and divisions, are ye not carnal, and walk as men?

** As we walk through this life, we allow the flesh to lead us in what we do rather than following the Holy Spirit's guidance! **

John 2: 23 – 25

23 Now when he was in Jerusalem at the passover, in the feast day, many believed in his name, when they saw the miracles which he did.

24 But Jesus did not commit himself unto them, because he knew all men,

25 And needed not that any should testify of man: for he knew what was in man.

** Read James chapter 2. James explains that it is by what Jesus did on the Cross that we are saved, but, because of being Saved, we want to do and we continue to do works for God as Jesus said [Matthew 28: 18 – 20], to go and be a Witness of Jesus Christ and tell everyone **what Jesus has done personally for you in your life and how**

**He leads and guides you by His Word
and the Holy Spirit in all that you do! ****

**I don't want to discourage you in your
walk with the LORD, I want to
encourage you to trust in Christ in all
things, Study His Word and tell all that
you meet, that you decern that Jesus
wants you to witness to about who and
what Jesus is to you!**

The Last Transition of Christ!

From the beginning, GOD Created Himself, a incorruptible body that can-not die, just like His Spirit, and named it Jesus! Through Jesus, He spoke everything into existence through Jesus Who became our Savior and LORD! Since GOD is Omni – Present and invisible, [**Colossians 1: 14 – 20] even the Angels would need to see Him sitting on God's Throne, [**Job 1: 6 & 2: 1]** ! Now, Let's make sure that you understand that there is only one God, [**Isaiah 43: 10 – 12**] and He works through the Trinity; The Father, Son & Holy Ghost ! [**Matthew 28: 18 – 20**]

These three are one! To truly know GOD, you must understand each of these and how and why they do what they do! As I have said before in other writings, We see GOD through the Love, Grace, Mercy and Forgiveness of Jesus; we see the Teaching, Guidance and Understanding through the Holy Spirit and we see the Authority and the giver of the Commandments & Statues that we **must** and will live by through the Father GOD ! Now, as we look at all these things, we realize that we have not seen the trees because of the Forest! To understand what the forest does and is about, we must take a look at each individual tree or Bible Story and as we understand each Bible Story, we start to understand the Bible! When we look at the Bible as a whole, we get confused like looking at a map. To find the right way to get to where you are going, you will need to look at the road in small sections so you can see all the obstacles and find the best and easiest way to travel to your destination! This is why God put these books in my heart to help others to look at who GOD is and what He wants us to do!

God's Word tells us that God came to the Jew first and then to the Gentile; [Romans 1: 16] and that God will return back to the Jew at the end of the Gentile age! **[Romans 11: 25 – 26] ****

Isaiah 40: 5 - 8

5 And the glory of the LORD shall be revealed, and all flesh shall see it together: for the mouth of the LORD hath spoken it.

⁶ The voice said, Cry. And he said, What shall I cry? All flesh is grass, and all the goodliness thereof is as the flower of the field:

⁷ The grass withereth, the flower fadeth: because the spirit of the LORD bloweth upon it: surely the people is grass.

⁸ The grass withereth, the flower fadeth: but **the word of our God shall stand for ever.**

Now, I said all that, to say this; We make transitions all the time in our lives! From a baby to a child, a teenager, a young adult to an older person! We know this in our bodies, but we also make transitions in our actions and way of thinking! But, we don't think about the transitions that GOD has made throughout time! I know that GOD said that He is the same yesterday, today and forever, but remaining the same GOD from the beginning, He has gone from an Invisible GOD to being Jesus Christ speaking all things into existence and sitting on the Throne of GOD to becoming Flesh, living and suffering the Cross here on earth as the Lamb of GOD, back to the Throne in Heaven to soon to return again to the earth as the Lion of Judah! Yet remaining GOD!

2 Peter 1: 12

[11] For so an entrance shall be ministered unto you abundantly into the everlasting kingdom of our Lord and Saviour Jesus Christ.

[12] Wherefore I will not be negligent to put you always in remembrance of these things, though ye know them, and be established in the present truth.

[13] Yea, I think it meet, as long as I am in this tabernacle, to stir you up by putting you in remembrance;

¹⁴ Knowing that shortly I must put off this my tabernacle, even as our Lord Jesus Christ hath shewed me.

** Now, the Truth has always been the Truth, but as time has gone by, we have learned through the Holy Spirit to see the Truth better than before! For an example; **Revelations 11: 1 – 9,** tells us that at the end times, that God will send His two witnesses back to earth and they will be killed and all the nations will see their bodies lying in the street for three and one half days! Back when I was a boy and studying God's Word, I couldn't figure out how all the nations could see this as it happened! Then when I was in grammar school they started to send monkeys into space. Then men went up and later man went to the moon! Satellites were placed in space and I started to understand through television that we could see what was happening anywhere in the world as it took place! Now, the Truth was the Truth, but I saw and understood a lot better than I did before!

As I study the Scriptures I see all these things that are happening now are leading up to a totally messed up world and how it is leading up to a one world government as the Scriptures tells us that the Anti-Christ will take control of! [Especially with the election of 2020 and how much fraud took place!] I matched a lot of what the Scriptures tells us to what has already happened and what I see coming to Scripture and I can tell you that Jesus is about to Call His Church up! [The Rapture] ! When this takes place, the Scriptures tells us that the Holy Spirit will turn back to the Jew [**Romans 1: 16]** from the Gentile! **[Romans 11: 25 – 32]** God has given us through **Rev. chapters 1 -4** the understanding of the 7 Church ages as to what God likes about the Churches and what God doesn't like about the Churches, so we can adapt to living the way God wants us to! Seeing that God says in **Rev. 3: 14 – 19** that we are in the last Church age of the Laodiceans and this Church makes God sick! If you have read my past four books, you will have seen how when Jesus calls us home, that He will turn back to the Jew! Right after the Rapture, the war of Gog-Magog [**Ezekiel ch. 38**] will take place! Notice how all of the nations that will come against Israel already has boots on the ground in that area except Gomer, [Germany] and they already have a treaty with Iran [Persia] to back them in war for selling Germany oil! There will be about four years [minimum] between the Rapture and the start of the Tribulations!

God's Word tells us that the Holy Ghost fell upon the Jew at the upper room in Acts 2: 1 – 4, then He turned to the Gentile through the seven Church Ages, [from the time of Jesus until the end of the Laodicean Church that started around 1900 when the Holy Ghost fell upon the

Gentiles at that time when the Holy Ghost revival started in California and went around the world! Notice how in Joel's prophesy in **Joel 2: 1 – 32** tells us that the Holy Ghost will fall again upon the Jew at the end days [after the first 3 ½ years of Tribulations] and there will be 144,000 Jews **[Rev. 14: 1 – 6]** will have their spiritual eyes opened and they will start to preach the Gospel of Jesus Christ and **Romans 11: 26** says that all of Israel will be saved! Then as we look at what God's Word says; We will see the **"Last Transition of Christ" as He comes back as the "Lion of Judah" and sets up the Throne of David where He will reign forever!****

 See my Bible Study about the 75 days of the Recompense of Christ !

<u>75 Days of the Recompence of Christ!</u>

Webster's Dictionary = Recompence:

1. To give Compensation to: Repay – to pay for;
2. To return in kind : Requite
3. An Equivalent or a return for something done, Suffered, or given: Compensation

I have studied the Scriptures since I was about ten years of age and I have studied the End Time ministry most of that time! God has shown me many things that I never heard any minister preach on and when I would speak to a minister about some of these things, they would either look at me like a new calf looking at a new gate or they would tell me that I just didn't understand or know what the Bible was saying! So, I spent most of my life studying, fasting and praying to seek God's understanding of what He was revealing to me in my studies and seeking a personal relationship with the Almighty GOD! I have written and published four books to date, and I speak to groups at every opportunity that God gives me and He opens doors for me to speak. I have always been intrigued with God's mathematics as He does all things through math and symbolism of numbers! One day as I was studying, I saw a relationship between the story in Daniel 12: 11 & 12 and Zechariah 14: 1 –

21; I did a little more research in the book of Revelation 19: 11 - 21 and found that as John was writing Revelations under the inspiration of the Holy Spirit, that he was informing us that at the end of time that not only would Jesus return back to earth onto the top of the Mount of Olives on a White Horse with those of us that had gone to Heaven in the calling away of the Church, [Rapture, 2nd 12 Elders] along with the Saints that had been Raptured at the Resurrection of Christ, [1st 12 Elders] riding on white horses behind Jesus Christ at His return!

Seeing all these Scriptures come together, there was an excitement stirring within me like I had not felt in a long time!   I started to run the numbers like I always had done and things began to open up to a whole new view of the

Trinity of GOD and I started to see GOD as I had never seen Him before! The Grace, Love and Mercy of God through Jesus Christ and the Guidance, Teaching and the Inspiration of the Holy Spirit! I also saw that The Father, being the Most High, was in fact the Creator and giver of the Commandments and Statues that we are to keep and follow throughout our lives! He's the one that people don't like to talk nor hear about! Man, [Flesh] doesn't like to be told what to do nor take orders from anyone!

Oops, that's off on another rabbit trail!

As I was saying, the numbers started to come together and I would like to show you the numbers on paper so you can understand what I am getting to!

Watch the numbers in Daniel 12, and **see why** the **Recompence** in Romans 11: 35

Daniel 12: 1 - 13

12 And at that time shall Michael stand up, the great prince which standeth for the children of thy people: and there shall be a time of trouble, such as never was since there was a nation even to that same time: and at that time thy people shall be delivered, every one that shall be found written in the book.

2 And many of them that sleep in the dust of the earth shall awake, some to everlasting life, and some to shame and everlasting contempt.

3 And they that be wise shall shine as the brightness of the firmament; and they that turn many to righteousness as the stars for ever and ever.

⁴ But thou, O Daniel, shut up the words, and seal the book, even to the time of the end: many shall run to and fro, and knowledge shall be increased.

⁵ Then I Daniel looked, and, behold, there stood other two, the one on this side of the bank of the river, and the other on that side of the bank of the river.

⁶ And one said to the man clothed in linen, which was upon the waters of the river, How long shall it be to the end of these wonders?

⁷ And I heard the man clothed in linen, which was upon the waters of the river, when he held up his right hand and his left hand unto heaven, and sware by him that liveth for ever that it shall be for **a time, times, and an half;** and when he shall have accomplished to scatter the power of the holy people, all these things shall be finished.

⁸ And I heard, but I understood not: then said I, O my Lord, what shall be the end of these things?

⁹ And he said, Go thy way, Daniel: for the words are closed up and sealed till the time of the end.

¹⁰ Many shall be purified, and made white, and tried; but the wicked shall do wickedly: and none of the wicked shall understand; but the wise shall understand.

¹¹ And from the time that the daily sacrifice shall be taken away, and the abomination that maketh desolate set up, there shall be a **thousand two hundred and ninety days.**

¹² Blessed is he that waiteth, and cometh to the **thousand three hundred and five and thirty days.**

[13] But go thou thy way till the end be: for thou shalt rest, and stand in thy lot at the end of the days.

Romans 11: 25 – 36

[25] For I would not, brethren, that ye should be ignorant of this mystery, lest ye should be wise in your own conceits; that **blindness in part is happened to Israel, until the fulness of the Gentiles be come in.**

[26] And **so all Israel shall be saved:** as it is written, **There shall come out of Sion the Deliverer, and shall turn away ungodliness from Jacob:**

[27] For this is my covenant unto them, when I shall take away their sins.

[28] As concerning the gospel, they are enemies for your sakes: but as touching

the election, they are beloved for the father's sakes.

²⁹ For the gifts and calling of God are without repentance.

³⁰ For as ye in times past have not believed God, yet have now obtained mercy through their unbelief:

³¹ Even so have these also now not believed, that through your mercy they also may obtain mercy.

³² For God hath concluded them all in unbelief, that he might have mercy upon all.

³³ O the depth of the riches both of the wisdom and knowledge of God! how unsearchable are his judgments, and his ways past finding out!

³⁴ For who hath known the mind of the Lord? or who hath been his counsellor?

[35] Or who hath first given to him, and it shall be **recompensed unto him again?**

[36] For of him, and through him, and to him, are all things: to whom be glory for ever. Amen.

Now; We know that the calendar that God gave Israel has only 360 days in a year, unlike ours, that has 364 except every forth year, [Leap Year] there is 365 days per year!

In looking at God's Word, I will always use the Calendar that God uses! There is 1,260 days in the 3 ½ years of Tribulations!

And two 3 ½ year periods to equal the 7 years of Tribulations!

So, in Daniel 12: we see in Vs. 11 that there will be 1,290 days until the end!

1,290 days – 1,260 days = 30 days over the 3 ½ years of the Great Tribulations. Then, Vs. 12 says that Blessed is he that waits to the 1,335 days ! that adds another 45 days to that number! So, 30 + 45 = 75 days past the seven years of Tribulations!   WHY!! Let's take a look at why!

Zechariah 14: 1 – 21

14 Behold, the day of the LORD cometh, and thy spoil shall be divided in the midst of thee.

² For I will gather all nations against Jerusalem to battle; and the city shall be taken, and the houses rifled, and the women ravished; and half of the city shall go forth into captivity, and the residue of the people shall not be cut off from the city.

******Rev. 19:11 – 16 ******

³ **Then shall the LORD go forth, and fight against those nations,** as when he fought in the day of battle.

⁴ **And his feet shall stand in that day upon the mount of Olives, which is before Jerusalem on the east, and the mount of Olives shall cleave in the midst thereof toward the east and toward the west, and there shall be a very great valley; and half of the mountain shall remove toward the north, and half of it toward the south.**

*****Rev. 16: 18 *****

⁵ And ye shall flee to the valley of the mountains; for the valley of the mountains shall reach unto Azal: yea, ye shall flee, like as ye fled from before the earthquake in the days of Uzziah king of Judah: and the LORD my God shall come, and all the saints with thee.

⁶ And it shall come to pass in that day, that the light shall not be clear, nor dark:

⁷ But it shall be one day which shall be known to the LORD, not day, nor night: but it shall come to pass, that at **evening time** it shall be light.

⁸ And it shall be in that day, that living waters shall go out from Jerusalem; half of them toward the former sea, and half of them toward the hinder sea: in summer and in winter shall it be.

⁹ And the LORD shall be king over all the earth: in that day shall there be one LORD, and his name one.

¹⁰ All the land shall be turned as a plain from Geba to Rimmon south of Jerusalem: and it shall be lifted up, and inhabited in her place, from Benjamin's gate unto the place of the first gate, unto the corner gate, and from the tower of Hananeel unto the king's winepresses.

¹¹ And men shall dwell in it, and there shall be no more utter destruction; but Jerusalem shall be safely inhabited.

¹² And this shall be the plague wherewith the LORD will smite all the people that have <u>fought against Jerusalem</u>; Their flesh shall consume away while they stand upon their feet, and their eyes shall consume away in their holes, and their tongue shall consume away in their mouth.

¹³ And it shall come to pass in that day, that a great tumult from the LORD shall be among them; and they shall lay hold every one on the hand of his neighbour, and his hand shall rise up against the hand of his neighbour.

¹⁴ And Judah also shall fight at Jerusalem; and the wealth of all the heathen round about shall be gathered together, gold, and silver, and apparel, in great abundance.

[15] And so shall be the plague of the horse, of the mule, of the camel, and of the ass, and of all the beasts that shall be in these tents, as this plague.

[16] And it shall come to pass, **that every one that is left of all the nations which came against Jerusalem** shall even go up from year to year to worship the King, the LORD of hosts, and to keep the feast of tabernacles.

[17] And it shall be, that whoso will not come up of all the families of the earth unto Jerusalem to worship the King, the LORD of hosts, even upon them shall be no rain.

[18] And if the family of Egypt go not up, and come not, that have no rain; there shall be the plague, wherewith the LORD will smite the heathen that come not up to keep the feast of tabernacles.

[19] This shall be the punishment of Egypt, and the punishment of all nations that

come not up to keep the feast of tabernacles.

²⁰ In that day shall there be upon the bells of the horses, HOLINESS UNTO THE LORD; and the pots in the LORD's house shall be like the bowls before the altar.

²¹ Yea, every pot in Jerusalem and in Judah shall be holiness unto the LORD of hosts: and all they that sacrifice shall come and take of them, and seethe therein: and in that day there shall be no more the Canaanite in the house of the LORD of hosts.

*** Notice, that after we have come back upon the back of white horses, riding behind our Lord Jesus Christ, that He has gotten off of His Big White Stallion and as His foot touches the ground, that there is an earthquake that splits the Mt. of Olives from East to West! [Rev. 16: 18 & Zech. 14: 4]. Now, all this takes place after Jesus's return to earth which is at the end of the seven years of Tribulations! The 75 days takes place after the Tribulations and Jesus's return as He sets up His Kingdom and Throne upon the Temple Mount as the Throne of David in the first 30 days per Daniel 12: 11, because those 30 days were included in Vs. 11. The Recompence takes place in the last 45 days per Daniel 12: 12, when Jesus speaks and all the people of the nations that came to fight against Israel shall be destroyed liken to a Nuclear Explosion! [Zechariah 14: 12]

After this Jesus is now on His Throne as the King of Kings and all the people that fought against Israel that are still alive will be required to travel to Jerusalem to worship Jesus Christ and keep the feast of tabernacles every year! [Zechariah 14: 16 – 19], and if they refuse to come to Jerusalem to worship Christ, there shall be no Rain fall upon their land and nation! [No Rain = No Food Crops], This is how it will be throughout the 1,000 yrs. Of the Millennial Reign! Satan will be bound in chains in the Pits of Hell, for a 1000 years, but the world will continue with children being born everyday! They are still of the flesh; and do sins of the flesh! We will be Ministers to the people and Jesus will still be on the Throne in Jerusalem! Read Chapter 20 of Revelations and see for yourself how bad people can be even without the help of Satan! When Satan is loosed he will get a multitude of people to follow him just before the Great White Throne Judgement!

Will you be ready to go in the Bride of Christ? [Wise Virgins]

Those that don't have their lives lined up with the Word of God and are filled with the Holy Spirit, [Foolish Virgins] will see a lot of these things take place until they are tested by giving their lives for their belief in Jesus Christ!

The time to decide and change our way of living is Now!

May GOD Bless you and show you the changes you need to make as you pray for the guidance of the Holy Spirit!

We are not hearing the Trumpets?

Jeremiah 6: 17
[17] **Also I set watchmen over you, saying, Hearken to the sound of the trumpet.** But they said, We will not hearken.

 **I believe that God is sounding Trumpets at the start of each happening that has taken place since Jesus left this earth until Jesus returns to this earth!
 We know that God works thru His numbers and seven [7] seems to be the number He is using. We know that seven [7] means completeness! God created all things in seven [7] days!

 God's Word says that there will be Seven years of tribulations and during that time there will be Seven Seals, Seven Trumpets, Seven Vials full of Plagues, Seven Thunders!!

The Seven Seals are opened by Jesus Christ only!! They are a time frame in which the events of the Seven Trumpets sound and the Seven Vials of God's wrath are poured out!!

The Seven Thunders were **not** to be written about!! I believe that they were something about the Seven Church Ages to come and John did write a little about them in Revelations, [Rev. chapters 2 & 3].

Now!!

God's Word says in I Thessalonians 4:16 that Jesus shall descend from heaven with a Shout, with the voice of the archangel, and with **the Trump of**

God and the dead in Christ shall rise first:

I Corinthians 15: 51 & 52 tells us;
51 Behold, I shew you a mystery; We shall not all sleep, but we shall all be changed, 52 In a moment, in the twinkling of an eye, **at the last trump:** for the trumpet shall sound, and the dead shall be raised incorruptible, and we shall be changed.

If there is a **Last Trumpet**, then there is a **First Trumpet** and more between them!

There are Seven Church Ages that are described by the Seven Candlesticks which represent the Seven Church Ages that is the Light of God's Word to His Church, [people] and the Seven Stars that represent the Seven Prophets that God sends His Word to us through;

Did we hear the Trumpets?

Did God sound trumpets with the four [4] Blood Moons in 1492, 1948 & 1967?

Has God sounded a trumpet with the four [4] Blood Moons that came in 2014 & 2015? Did we hear them?

I believe that **GOD sounded a Big Trumpet in around 1900,** when the Holy Ghost fell on the Church in California at the school where Charles Parham's students went into a room upstairs at the school and in groups rotating their time, they Fasted and Prayed for twenty four hours a day until the Holy Ghost fell upon them [Acts 2: 1-4], and they came out speaking in tongues! **GOD had restored the Apostolic Faith back to the**

Church! William Seymour was working at the school and asked to learn more about GOD, and after the HG had fallen upon them it spread into the city when Seymour cleaned out an old stable barn and started preaching the gospel! The HG was moving quickly and other ministers like John G. Lake joined the movement before he went to Africa where God spread the Apostolic Message around the world! Please read Church History! The Laodicean Church, [Rev. 3: 14-22] had begun!

God sounded another loud Trumpet in 1948 when Israel became a nation again! And again in 1967 at the six day war when Israel took control of the whole city of Jerusalem and the Temple Mount of Solomon's Temple!

There have been many Trumpets sounding as this Last Church Age approaches the "Calling away of the Church! [Rapture] such as in 2020 when President Trump moved America's Embassy from Tele vie to Jerusalem and acknowledged Jerusalem as the Capital of Israel!

With all that is happening now in Washington and around the world, we see that all the Scriptures of the End Times are coming to pass and things are setting this world up for the people to start calling for a one world leader! Just as God's Word foretells us it would be! I explain this more in detail in my first book, "Beyond the Rapture"! The

Churches are doing exactly what God's Word says they would do. [Rev. 3: 14-22] Laid back and warm! Not Hot nor Cold! They come to Church on Sunday and live for the Cares of this world, [Luke 21: 34] rather than studying God's Word and Witnessing to people as Jesus told us to do! **"That's our Job!"** [Matthew 28: 19-20]

God created us to make Choices about how we would live and where we would spend Eternity, Heaven or Hell, it's your choice! Wise Virgin in the Bride or Foolish Virgin going into the Great Tribulations to die for our belief in Jesus Christ as our Lord and GOD!

Are you seeking GOD through Jesus Christ and the guidance of the Holy Spirit in your life? If so, you will study, pray and fast to show yourself approved, [Tim. 2: 15],

Don't get me wrong! None of us will be Saved by any means except because of what Jesus did on **The Cross!!!** But [Luke 21: 36] tells us to Watch & Pray that we are accounted worthy to escape all these things that shall come to pass and stand before the Son of Man!

Are you hearing this Trumpet sounding to and for You?

There is still a Chance!

God tells us everything we need to know about everything that happened in the past, present and future. The Scripture says, " Study to show yourselves approved, a workman, not being ashamed, but rightly dividing the Scriptures". God tells us that, so we would understand how to study and research the Word to find Scriptures that explain other Scriptures. As I read the book of Revelations, I understand that God is explaining to us in Revelation 2 & 3, through the Seven Church Ages, that there are things that we are doing, that are pleasing to Him, and things that He does not want us to do! The first Christian Church was "Ephesus"; They had done good, but God told them that they had left their first love! Do you remember when you first got Saved? How you loved God so much, and how you wanted to tell [Witness] everybody about what God had done for you and how much you loved Him! Just like "Ephesus" the Church today has mostly left their first love! They pay the Pastors to do the witnessing and the spreading of the Word on television and they have stopped being a witness for God! They don't worship in the Spirit anymore! God said; John 4: 24;   "God is a Spirit: and they that worship Him must worship Him in Spirit and in Truth."

With each Church Age, God tells us how He wants " The Church" to live and look like! He told us in each Church Age, the things that we should not do, like with **the Fourth Church Age, "Thyatira". God tells us that we should not be Tolerant of wrong doings [Sin] and not to keep silent when our Government goes against the Word of God! We are to speak up and rebuke those that sin or " just go along with it". We should also Pray for our leaders and Brothers and Sisters in Christ!**

Now here's the Rub!

God knows the End from the Beginning and He knows Exactly what the Last Church Age will look like!

God's Word tells us that in the last Church Age; "Laodiceans", The people would straddle the fence! They will not get "Hot" for God, [Witnessing and living per the Word] nor will they get "cold" [Quit]! God says that they will be "Luke Warm", and He will spue them out of His mouth! [Vomit] The Church of today makes God sick! He tells us what we must change.

Revelations 3: 18

18 I counsel thee to buy of me **gold** tried in the fire, that thou mayest be rich; and **white raiment**, that thou mayest be clothed, and that the shame of thy nakedness do not appear; and anoint thine eyes with **eye salve**, that thou mayest see.

19 As many as I love, I rebuke and chasten: be zealous therefore, and repent.

I Peter 1: 7

7 That the trial of your **faith,** being much more precious than of **gold** that perisheth, though it be tried with fire, might be found unto praise and honour and glory at the appearing of Jesus Christ:

Proverbs 23: 23

23 Buy the truth, and sell it not; also wisdom, and instruction, and understanding.

Revelation 19: 8

8 And to her was granted that she should be arrayed in fine linen, clean and white: for the **fine linen is the righteousness of saints.**

Romans 8: 29

²⁹ For whom he did foreknow, he also did predestinate to be conformed to the image of his Son, that he might be the firstborn among many brethren.

John 14: 19

¹⁹ Yet a little while, and the world seeth me no more; **but ye see me:** because I live, ye shall live also.

All this will Cost Us Something!!!

Seek, and ye shall find; Knock, and the door will be opened;

Ask, and it will be given!

Jesus tells us in Matthew 25: 1-13

Then shall the kingdom of heaven be likened unto ten virgins, which took their lamps, and went forth to meet the bridegroom.

2 And five of them were wise, and five were foolish.

3 They that were foolish took their lamps, and took no oil with them:

4 But the wise took oil in their vessels with their lamps.

5 While the bridegroom tarried, they all slumbered and slept.

6 And at midnight there was a cry made, Behold, the bridegroom cometh; go ye out to meet him.

7 Then all those virgins arose, and trimmed their lamps.

8 And the foolish said unto the wise, Give us of your oil; for our lamps are gone out.

[9] But the wise answered, saying, Not so; lest there be not enough for us and you: but go ye rather to them that sell, and buy for yourselves.

[10] And while they went to buy, the bridegroom came; and they that were ready went in with him to the marriage: and the door was shut.

[11] Afterward came also the other virgins, saying, Lord, Lord, open to us.

[12] But he answered and said, Verily I say unto you, I know you not.

[13] Watch therefore, for ye know neither the day nor the hour wherein the Son of man cometh.

Remember; They were all Virgins! They were Pure and Clean!

5 Virgins were ready for the Marriage [Rapture], and 5 Virgins were Not ready! Their Lamps, [Vessels, Souls] were not filled with Oil [Holy Ghost], Their

Wicks [Lives] were not trimmed [Lined up with the Word], They were not shining their light [Witnessing]!

Isaiah 54: 1

Sing, O barren, thou that didst not bear; break forth into singing, and cry aloud, thou that didst not travail with child: for more are the children of the desolate than the children of the **married wife,** saith the LORD.

God is saying that at the time of the "Rapture" there will be more people that are saved, that will live and go into the "Tribulation Period" than those that go in the "Bride"

Again, I say, They were all Virgins!!! [Saved]

Luke 21: 36

[34] And take heed to yourselves, lest at any time your hearts be overcharged with surfeiting, and drunkenness, and

cares of this life, and so that day come upon you unawares.

³⁵ For as a snare shall it come on all them that dwell on the face of the whole earth.

³⁶ Watch ye therefore, and pray always, that ye may be **accounted worthy** to escape all these things that shall come to pass, and to stand before the Son of man.

I am not writing this to scare you, I want to warn you to forget all this other foolishness and live your lives, But, keep your minds upon God through Jesus Christ and live those lives based upon the Word of God! Jesus said that He was coming back for those that were <u>Diligently seeking Him!</u> John the Baptist was warning the people that, The time of the Messiah was come and for them to get ready! I am doing the same thing!!!

What God is saying is not easy for this Church to hear! Just like the first

Church, "Ephesus". God allowed them to be hung on crosses, tied to poles and wrapped in sacks, soaked in oil and set on fire and the burned to death! They died in the Roman Coliseum by Gladiators and wild beast!! God will allow you to be saved and bound for heaven, but He is coming back for a "Bride" that has prepared herself and is ready! Are you one of those? Those that have not kept His Word and continued to "Watch and Pray" will miss the "Calling away of the Church, [Rapture], and will die in the Tribulations!

Revelation 7: 14

13 And one of the elders answered, saying unto me, What are these which are arrayed in white robes? and whence came they?

14 And I said unto him, Sir, thou knowest. And he said to me, **These are they which came out of great tribulation, and have washed their**

**robes, and made them white in the
blood of the Lamb.**

¹⁵ Therefore are they before the throne of
God, and serve him day and night in his
temple: and he that sitteth on the throne
shall dwell among them.

The Problem, as I have warned many
pastors and ministers is, because they
worry about the people's feelings and
about numbers and money, They are
leading God's Children into the
Tribulations!! This, They will answer to
God for!!

Isaiah 56: 10-11

¹⁰ **His watchmen** are blind: they are all
ignorant, they are all dumb dogs, they
cannot bark; sleeping, lying down,
loving to slumber.

¹¹ Yea, they are greedy dogs which can
never have enough, and they are
shepherds that cannot understand:

they all look to their own way, **every one for his gain, from his quarter.**

12 Come ye, say they, I will fetch wine, and we will fill ourselves with strong drink; and tomorrow shall be as this day, and much more abundant.

God told Israel to place "Watchmen" upon the walls to keep watch and to cry out a warning to the people if danger was approaching!

Acts 20: 9 – 10

9 And there sat in a window a certain young man named Eutychus, being fallen into a deep sleep: and as Paul was long preaching, he sunk down with sleep, and fell down from the third loft, and was taken up dead.

10 And Paul went down, and fell on him, and embracing him said, Trouble not yourselves; for his life is in him.

Like Eutychus, The Church of the "Laodiceans" are half in and half out and will fall. But, there is still a chance of redemption! First of all, it is up to you to make that choice and do what I have already shown you above! Also, the Ministers must do as Paul did, and throw themselves upon the mercy of God in Prayer and Fasting for God to help us preach the solid and truth of the Gospel of Jesus Christ as we warn the people of His soon coming!!!

We must align our lives with the Word of God. **Don't misunderstand me, We are saved, only by the Blood of Jesus Christ that was shed for our redemption and what He did on the Cross!** Jesus said, "If you love me, you will keep my commandments".

John 1: 1

1 In the beginning was the Word, and the Word was with God, and the Word was God.

[14] And the Word was made flesh, and dwelt among us, (and we beheld his glory, the glory as of the only begotten of the Father,) full of grace and truth.

Beloved of GOD, I beg you to turn away from those Idols, [Sports, Materials, ect.] everything that takes your mind off of GOD, For God is the only one or thing that is worthy of your Praise! Time is Short! God made you a creature of choice, You alone will choose Heaven or Hell; - Rapture or Tribulations!!!

Choose well my friend, Choose Well !

How the Church got off of the "True Rock Foundation" that Jesus said, "Upon this Rock, I will build My Church"!

I would like to explain today, How the Church that Jesus said that He would build, got off the "Solid Rock Foundation" that Jesus [GOD] taught to the Disciples Himself!

Jeremiah 2: 7 – 13

[7] And I brought you into a plentiful country, to eat the fruit thereof and the goodness thereof; but when ye entered, ye defiled my land, and made mine heritage an abomination.

[8] **The priests said not, Where is the LORD?** and they that handle the law knew me not: **the pastors also transgressed against me**, and the prophets prophesied by Baal, and walked after things that do not profit.

[9] Wherefore I will yet plead with you, saith the LORD, and with your children's children will I plead.

[10] For pass over the isles of Chittim, and see; and send unto Kedar, and consider diligently, and see if there be such a thing.

[11] **Hath a nation changed their gods,** which are yet no gods? **but my people have changed their glory for that which doth not profit.**

[12] Be astonished, O ye heavens, at this, and be horribly afraid, be ye very desolate, saith the LORD.

¹³ For my people have committed two evils; they have forsaken me the fountain of living waters, and hewed them out cisterns, broken cisterns, that can hold no water.

I want to explain to you, that I am **not** putting down any Church, nor anyone that is a follower of Christ! If you are trying to live a Christian life, then we are Brothers and Sisters in Christ our Lord! I want you to see through history and the Bible, how over time, Satan, through the desire of the flesh and the spirit of man, has perverted and misguided the Church to lead us away from that "Solid Rock Foundation" that Jesus established for the Church to live by and teach!

You know, I don't know why GOD didn't just kill all of mankind and start over, the way God started to do with the

Children of Israel in the desert, [Exodus 32: 10-14], when Moses begged GOD to remember His covenant with Father Abraham! [Gen. 15:18]! GOD had already destroyed the world with water at the flood and started over with Noah, so why doesn't GOD destroy mankind now?

GOD's Word tells us that He said that He knew us before the foundation of the world! He knew then what mankind would do! We don't even know who GOD truly is! We know the Love, Grace and Mercy of GOD through Jesus the Christ and we know the Teaching and Guidance of the Holy Spirit, but, We have overlooked who GOD the Father is because, to know the Father, we must know that He has made Rules like His **Commandants and Statues** the we must live by, and we don't want to be ruled by anyone, except ourselves!

GOD doesn't want to Rule us, He just wants us to do what His Word tells us, because it is best for us and our lives will be much better! But No! we want to do what we want to do, the way we want to do it! So, [Isaiah 28: 9-12], we look for Preachers that will give us that warm and fuzzy feeling when we go to Church! Preachers seem to be looking for more people and bigger offerings, more than saving Souls in this day and time!

I have told many of the Pastor friends of mine, that I am just Crazy enough to believe that if we had 100 people in the Church and lost 90 of them, that GOD would bless the other 10 people that are diligently seeking Him to the point that the Church's needs would be met, financially and Spiritually with those few that stay in Prayer and Fasting!

Because of our desires, we have watered down the Gospel to fit our wants! [Isaiah 28: 9-12], So, GOD doesn't work in the Church very much anymore! GOD works in the individual lives of those that are diligently seeking Him!

We need to remember that GOD is GOD! He is a Sovereign GOD! He does what He wants to do and no one nor anything can stop Him or do anything about what He does or says!

[Daniel 2: 21 & 4: 32] But, GOD loves us, "His Creation" and He knows that we are more than a spirit, because He put our spirit into flesh, that we will be weak and are subject to follow after the flesh that is apt to do as it wants. GOD created us to be creatures of choice, and He allows us to choose, [Isaiah 28: 9 – 12], what we will believe and do. He has given us His Word to lead us and His Spirit [Holy Spirit] within us to guide us, if we choose to follow Him and do His will for us! GOD wants us to choose the right way, but He will allow us to do whatever we want to do! GOD's Word tells us that we can live for Him or we can choose not to. What have you chosen to do? When this life is over, will you have chosen Heaven or Hell!

You see, the Church is no more than a group of people. It's not the building. It's not the organization. It is a group of people made up of individuals, like yourselves, that choose to follow GOD, [The Word; John 1:1] and do what He ask us to do. There is only two ways to do anything, the right way [God's way] or the wrong way [Satan's way]. What way do you choose? Remember, the spirit is willing, but, the flesh is weak! As we look at the Church, we see that the flesh has taken control of the system and made it [Again: Isaiah 28: 9-12], into what and the way the flesh wants it to be! GOD's Word has given us an understanding of what will be going on at the end, just before Jesus the Christ steps out into the clouds and the trumpet sounds and Jesus calls His Children home! If you are not watching what is happening, [Luke 21:36] then you will not be ready, [Matthew 24: 1-14]! I am not writing this to scare you **nor am I condemning you**. I am only doing what GOD has called me to do as a Minister of the Gospel, [Ephesians 4: 11 – 13]. Now, once we discover that the Church is off of the "Solid Rock Foundation" that Jesus established when He was here, [Matthew 13 – 19], what do we do about it? I can not change the system that is established and not teaching the "Full Truth", [2

Peter 1: 12] but Lynn and I can have a Bible Study at our home, as we do and help others to see and allow the Holy Spirit to do what Jesus said, [John 14: 26]. If we teach you how to return back to that "Solid Rock Foundation" and you teach others, and they teach more. Then we will all begin to Worship GOD, the way that the Church did before, [Jeremiah 6:16] [Isaiah 30: 20-21] and the established system will be changed!!!

Let me explain about Jonathan Edwards and Henry Ward Beecher!

In the mid 1700s a pastor named Jonathan Edwards spoke to a Church in the state of Massachusetts that the pastor had told him that the people there was "Cold and Spiritually Dead"! History tells us that Edwards walked upon the platform and fixed his eyes on the back of the Church and began to preach! Edwards told them that God's Word says that God knew us before the beginning of the world and so, if God knew that we would never choose to accept Jesus Christ as our Lord, he said, then tell me why God doesn't cut the thread of life that holds you in this life, pull the curtain back between you and Hell, let you take your last breath, die and burn in Hell forever!!!

That sermon was called, "Sinners in the hands of an Angry GOD"! It is still taught in ministry to and it started a fire in the people there and they began to moan and groan and run for the Alter to pray for God's Mercy!

That type of preaching started what is known as the "Great North East Awakening" and spread over five [5] States!

What a Great Revival!

Then in the mid 1800s a man named Henry Ward Beecher was pastor of a Church in New York where he was known to speak so elegant and all about the Love of Christ, with a twist of Warm Fuzzy Fillings that the people loved to hear him speak! Henry taught the people that there is no "Fear of GOD" and the Church started to change until 1900 when a small group of Bible students started to fast and pray for another "Upper Room Experience". That is when the Laodicean Church began! What I am telling you is that the "Flesh" will continually fight to change the Word of GOD to make it fit the life style that we want to live!

Let's, take a look at what has happened to the Church through- out history!

The Doctrine of the Nicolaitans !

I want you to understand what happened in history when the First Roman Church changed their structure and their belief of how to worship! They turned their restructure over to a group of men that like most men have a desire to be Boss! This group looked at the Church as an opportunity to gain some power and control over the people. They knew it was growing by leaps and bounds and would be out of control, [in their minds]. see the lack of Faith? They didn't understand that God was in it and He had control! God was calling men to labor in His Church and he had established how He would work in them! [Ephesians 4:11-13]. Let's look at what took place.

<u>Revelations 2: 6 & 15 -------GOD hates it !</u>

[6] But this thou hast, that thou hatest the deeds of the Nicolaitanes, which I also hate.

[15] So hast thou also them that hold the doctrine of the Nicolaitanes, which thing I hate.

<u>Nicolaitane = Greek =</u>

<u>Nikao – To Conquer !</u>

<u>Lao – The Laity !</u>

Elders, [Presbyters] = Older Men w/ Christian Experience !

Overseers, [Bishops] = Office of these Men !

Acts 20: 17 – 28

¹⁷ And from Miletus he sent to Ephesus, and called the elders of the church.

¹⁸ And when they were come to him, he said unto them, Ye know, from the first day that I came into Asia, after what manner I have been with you at all seasons,

¹⁹ Serving the LORD with all humility of mind, and with many tears, and temptations, which befell me by the lying in wait of the Jews:

²⁰ And how I kept back nothing that was profitable unto you, but have shewed you, and have taught you publicly, and from house to house,

²¹ Testifying both to the Jews, and also to the Greeks, repentance toward God, and faith toward our Lord Jesus Christ.

^{22} And now, behold, I go bound in the spirit unto Jerusalem, not knowing the things that shall befall me there:

^{23} Save that the Holy Ghost witnesseth in every city, saying that bonds and afflictions abide me.

^{24} But none of these things move me, neither count I my life dear unto myself, so that I might finish my course with joy, and the ministry, which I have received of the Lord Jesus, to testify the gospel of the grace of God.

^{25} And now, behold, I know that ye all, among whom I have gone preaching the kingdom of God, shall see my face no more.

^{26} Wherefore I take you to record this day, that I am pure from the blood of all men.

^{27} For I have not shunned to declare unto you all the counsel of God.

^{28} Take heed therefore unto yourselves, and to all the flock, over the which the Holy Ghost hath made you overseers, to feed the church of God, which he hath purchased with his own blood.

Matthew 20: 25 – 28

^{25} But Jesus called them unto him, and said, Ye know that the princes of the Gentiles exercise dominion over them, and they that are great exercise authority upon them.

^{26} But it shall not be so among you: but whosoever will be great among you, let him be your minister;

^{27} And whosoever will be chief among you, let him be your servant:

^{28} Even as the Son of man came not to be ministered unto, but to minister, and to give his life a ransom for many.

Matthew 23: 1 – 9

1 Then spake Jesus to the multitude, and to his disciples,

² Saying The scribes and the Pharisees sit in Moses' seat:

³ All therefore whatsoever they bid you observe, that observe and do; but do not ye after their works: for they say, and do not.

⁴ For they bind heavy burdens and grievous to be borne, and lay them on men's shoulders; but they themselves will not move them with one of their fingers.

⁵ But all their works they do for to be seen of men: they make broad their phylacteries, and enlarge the borders of their garments,

⁶ And love the uppermost rooms at feasts, and the chief seats in the synagogues,

⁷ And greetings in the markets, and to be called of men, Rabbi, Rabbi.

⁸ But be not ye called Rabbi: for one is your Master, even Christ; and all ye are brethren.

⁹ And call no man your father upon the earth: for one is your Father, which is in heaven.

Revelation 13: 3

³ And I saw one of his heads as it were wounded to death; and his deadly wound was healed: and all the world wondered after the beast.

Now we know by history that the head was the Pagan Roman Empire; that great world political power. That head rose again to be the Roman Catholic Spiritual empire.

When this redirection from the " Rock Foundation" that Jesus established and taught to the Disciples that became the Apostle's Creed crept into the Church, men began to a place in the office of Bishop with the result that this position was being given to the more Educated and Materially-Progressive and Politically Minded men ! Human Knowledge and Program began to take over Divine Wisdom's place and The Holy Spirit no longer controlled! This was a tragic and evil event because the bishops began to believe that it no longer required a Calling from GOD to minister the Word and the understanding of what God wanted for His people. This allowed evil men [seducers] to direct the Church with their desires and needs! This allowed them to do what they wanted to do! This led to how were they going to advance higher in power and structure of the church! So, they gave themselves titles and formed higher positions in the church and led to a religious hierarchy; They formed Archbishops over the bishops and Cardinals over the archbishops and then there came the Pope, who they think stands equal to Christ!

What with the Nicolaitan doctrine and the restructure of Christian structure that Jesus taught us while He was here. The results had to be what Ezekiel saw in chapter 8: 10,

¹⁰ So I went in and saw; and behold every form of creeping things, and abominable beasts, and all the idols of the house of Israel, portrayed upon the wall round about.

Revelation 18: 2

² And he cried mightily with a strong voice, saying, Babylon the great is fallen, is fallen, and is become the habitation of devils, and the hold of every foul spirit, and a cage of every unclean and hateful bird, for all nations have drunk of the wine of the wrath of her fornications.

They took over the minds and lives of the people and made them the servants of a denominational doctrine and creeds!

Read the edict of Theodosius X.

Theodosius' First Edict.

This edict was issued immediately after he was baptized by the First Church of Rome.

"We three emperors will that our subjects steadfastly adhere to the religion which was taught by Saint Peter to the Romans, which has been faithfully preserved by tradition and which is now professed by the pontiff, Damasus of Rome, and Peter, bishop of Alexandria, a man of Apostolic holiness according to the institution of the Apostles, and the doctrine of the Gospel; Let us believe in one Godhead of the Father, Son, and the Holy Spirit, of equal majesty in the Holy Trinity. We order that the adherents of this faith be called Catholic Christians; We brand all the senseless followers of the other religions with the infamous name of heretics, and forbid their conventicles assuming the name of churches. Besides the condemnation of divine justice, guided by heavenly wisdom shall think proper to inflict…"

The fifteen penal laws that this emperor issued in as many years deprived the evangelicals of all rights to the exercise of their religion, excluded them from all civil offices, and threatened them with fines, confiscation, banishment and even in some cases , death !

The Bible and history tells us that God said that she was a Harlot and had daughters! Read Revelations chapter 18 !

Ephesians 4: 1 – 19

I therefore, the prisoner of the Lord, beseech you that ye walk worthy of the vocation wherewith ye are called,

2 With all lowliness and meekness, with longsuffering, forbearing one another in love;

3 Endeavouring to keep the unity of the Spirit in the bond of peace.

4 *There is* one body, and one Spirit, even as ye are called in one hope of your calling;

5 One Lord, one faith, one baptism,

6 One God and Father of all, who *is* above all, and through all, and in you all.

7 But unto every one of us is given grace according to the measure of the gift of Christ.

8 Wherefore he saith, When he ascended up on high, he led captivity captive, and gave gifts unto men.

9 (Now that he ascended, what is it but that he also descended first into the lower parts of the earth?

10 He that descended is the same also that ascended up far above all heavens, that he might fill all things.)

11 And he gave some, apostles; and some, prophets; and some, evangelists; and some, pastors and teachers;

12 For the perfecting of the saints, for the work of the ministry, for the edifying of the body of Christ:

13 Till we all come in the unity of the faith, and of the knowledge of the Son of God, unto a perfect man, unto the

measure of the stature of the fulness of
Christ:

14 That we *henceforth* be no more
children, tossed to and fro, and carried
about with every wind of doctrine, by the
sleight of men, *and* cunning craftiness,
whereby they lie in wait to deceive;

15 But speaking the truth in love, may
grow up into him in all things, which is
the head, *even* Christ:

16 From whom the whole body fitly
joined together and compacted by that
which every joint supplieth, according to
the effectual working in the measure of
every part, maketh increase of the body
unto the edifying of itself in love.

17 This I say therefore, and testify in the
Lord, that ye henceforth walk not as
other Gentiles walk, in the vanity of their
mind,

18 Having the understanding darkened, being alienated from the life of God through the ignorance that is in them, because of the blindness of their heart:

19 Who being past feeling have given themselves over unto lasciviousness, to work all uncleanness with greediness.

Jesus explained in Matthew 28: 18-20 to Baptist in the **name** of the Father, Son and Holy Ghost; Then Peter tells us in Acts 2: 38, that name! Jesus Christ!

Oh! How the Church has changed! Please seek GOD through the name of Jesus which is the Word in Flesh! John 1:1 – 14!

The Doctrine of Balaam

I would like to explain to you about the Doctrine of Balaam that goes along with The Nicolaiane layout of the Church!

Jesus Christ gave the us the layout of how the Church should be operated in Ephesians 4: 11 – 13, when He explained through Paul to the Ephesians that God gave the Church. These were not titles of progression upward in the Church, but names of the types of Ministers that work together to Perfect the Saints in their maturity from babes to full adults in Christ! [Eph. 4: 11-13; Hebrews 5: 12-14]. God didn't call Ministers to rent the flock to become rich and filled with Pride, walking about like they were something to behold! Lording over the people of God! Teaching the Scriptures in little stories that make people feel good about themselves and get them to give money to the Church so the pastors can live high on the hog! I am not judging you pastors, but you will stand before Jesus Christ and explain what you did and what you didn't do! [Feed the Flock meat in due season!]. We are in the time of John the Baptist! We need to be Perfecting the five Foolish Virgins that attend our Churches that are not ready to go in the Rapture! Why do you think that Jesus told that parable to us? Stop playing Church, you should know the Time! Are we not the "Sons of Issachar? [I Chronicles 12: 32].

Let's look a little closer at this!

Revelation 2: 14

14 But I have a few things against thee, because thou hast there them that hold the doctrine of Balaam, who taught Balac to cast a stumblingblock before the children of Israel, to eat things sacrificed unto idols, and to commit fornication.

Now you just can't have a Nicolaiane set-up in the church and not have this other doctrine come in too. If you take away the Word of God and the moving of the Spirit as a means of worship, [They that worship me must worship me in Spirit and Truth]. Then you have to give the people another form of worship as a substitute, and substitution spells Balaamism!

If we are going to understand what the doctrine of Balaam is in the New Testament Church, we had better go back and see what it was in the Old Testament Church!

The story is found in Numbers chapter 22-25. Now we know that Israel was the chosen people of God and they were like the Pentecostals of their day. They had taken refuge under the Blood,[on the door post] and had been baptized in the Red Sea and came out singing and dancing in the Spirit. So Israel came to the borders of Moab and ask to pass through their land. They said that they would pay for any grass eaten by their animals and for any damage they may cause! Now Balak their king had no intent of letting Israel pass through their country and knew that he could make money out of this deal! The king went to a prophet named Balaam and asked him to make a deal. Now Balaam was only to glad to do this as he wanted make some money and to take part in political affairs and have power over the people!

"Doesn't that sound just like what is going on in our Country right now!"

Democrats seem to want to curse everyone that won't go their way on everything !

Balaam asked and God said NO! Balaam went back to Balak and Balak offered more money and power and honor! Balaam went back to God and asked again and God saw his perversity and told him to go. Balaam got on his donkey and went.

Just like the people in the Church today, they still don't understand that God is One God and the Trinity is the different titles that God works through! They still baptize in three titles, [Matthew 28: 19-20], instead of in the **name of Jesus, [Acts 2: 38]!** They don't worship in the Spirit, don't believe in speaking in tongues nor dancing before the LORD anymore!!! And I'm talking about Pentecostal Churches! And they think that they are all right! **"That's Balaamites"**

See the doctrine of Balaam! Go ahead anyway, Do it your way! They say " Well, God has blessed us, it must be alright." [Isaiah 28: 9 – 12],[" Precept upon precept"], They perceive the Scriptures to mean what they want them to mean so they can live the life style that they want to live and feel good about it and little by little they change [Water down] the Gospel of Jesus Christ to suit themselves! I know that God blessed you, I don't deny that. But it's still the same organizational route that Balaam took. It's defiance to God's Word, It's false teaching!

So Balaam went down the road until the angel stood in the road in his way. That prophet [bishop, cardinal, chairman, president and general overseer] was so blinded to the Spiritual things by the thought of honor and glory and money that he could not see the angel with his sword drawn. The little donkey saw him and dodged back and forth until he finally crushed Balaam's foot against a stone wall. The donkey stopped and would not go on. So Balaam jumped off and started to beat him. That's when God gave that donkey a tongue to speak. The donkey said to Balaam, "Am I not your donkey and haven't I carried you faithfully?" Balaam said, you are my donkey and have carried me faithfully until now; God has always spoken in a tongue. He spoke at Belshazzar's feast and then at Pentecost. He is doing it again today! It's a warning of soon coming judgement! Then the angel was made visible to Balaam. He told Balaam that except for the donkey, he would be dead now for tempting God. But when Balaam promised to go back, he was sent on with the admonition to say only what God gave him to say! So Balaam killed a ram, signifying the coming of the Messiah. He knew how to come before GOD! He had the mechanics just right;

but not the Dynamics; same as now. Can't you see it, Nicolaitanes? Doctrines and creeds won't get you anywhere. It can't take the place of Manifestation of the Spirit! That is what happened at Nicaea. They putt over Balaam's Doctrine, not the Doctrine of Jesus Christ. After the sacrifice was made, Balaam was ready to prophecy. God tied his tongue so he could not curse Israel but only bless them!

Balak got so mad but you can't argue with GOD!, Signs and Wonders followed the Church after 1900 when the Laodicean Church Age started; they were vindicated – not in themselves , but in GOD! God didn't have any respect for those Nicolaitanes, [Read Rev. 2: 1-7], but He did have respect for the

Pentecostal Churches for they had the Word vindicated amongst them.

Moab looked down on Israel just as the big organizations looked down on small churches that were Spirit filled and say "How unruly and unorganized they are"! Now Balaam knew that if he could get Israel to sin, God would kill them! He invited them to a party. Have you ever heard of "Guilty by Association"! Why do we not teach about **Sanctification anymore, God said that we are set apart!** So they came and as they watched the sexy Moabitish women dance their little dance and undress as they whirled around doing their thing, the Lust rose up in the Israelites and they were drawn into adultery, and GOD in wrath slew forty-two thousand of them!

Where is the "Fear of the LORD" in our Churches? [Proverbs 1: 7]

Constantine did this at Nicaea and after Nicaea. They invited the people to convention. And when the church sat down to eat, and rose up to play [partaking of church form, ceremonies, and pagan feast named after Christian rites], she was trapped; she had committed fornication. And GOD walked out!

Don't get caught up into these doctrines and creeds that take you away from the True Word of GOD! Or anything else that don't line up with the Word of GOD and the Spirit, or you will be dead, just like the rest of these churches that God said would come in the Last Days per 2 Thessalonians 2:3

and Revelations 3: 14-19; I am not
saying to stop going to church, but Stay
With The Word of GOD! Worship Him in
the Spirit!

In Closing!

As I come to the close of this book, it has always been my greatest desire to preach and teach the Word of GOD to people that are tired of playing Church! The Time of Christ's return is drawing very near as anyone that studies God's Word will tell you. Just as GOD killed and destroyed the world in Noah's day and in the days of Sodom & Gomorrah, God found just a few people that he saved from what came upon this world, just as it will be soon at the Calling away of the Church! I pray that you will be ready, [Wise Virgins], because it is coming whether we believe it or not!

Also, as I have said, God has had His hand on me all my life even throughout my teenaged rebellion years. I thank

God that he brought me to a Church where I heard a Pastor and Brother in Christ, that I believe to be the Prophet to this Church age, [Laodicean Church], Brother William M. Branham!

Through his and other pastors in the Apostolic Faith's Churches, I became the Christian that I am today! It is only by what Jesus did on the Cross that we are saved, but we were saved to do good works! God the "Father" gave us Commandments and Statutes that He demands that we keep and we do the best that we can and know that God looks at the heart, [Proverbs 3: 1-6; 21: 2], and leads and guides us by the Holy Spirit down the paths that God wants us to follow!

It is my prayer that you have been Blessed and have had your eyes opened to the "Present Truth" [2 Peter 1: 12] with a fuller understanding about what time we are living in and how to start allowing the Holy Spirit to reveal the "Stories inside the Stories" of God's Word. [Romans 15: 4; & 1 Corinthians 10: 11].

May GOD Bless you and Keep you!

Sincerely

Red Jackson

Notes

Notes

Notes